Presented To:

Dennis

Presented By:

Joyce

May reading this book help
you daily in your
desire to grow closer
with God.

Date:

Father's Day
2003

GOD'S LITTLE LESSONS
FOR DADS

Honor Books

God's Little Lessons for Dads
ISBN # 1-56292-694-2
Copyright © 1999, 2003 by Honor Books
An Imprint of Cook Communications Ministries
4050 Lee Vance View
Colorado Springs, CO 80918

Some devotions drawn from original manuscripts prepared by W. B. Freeman Concepts, Inc., Tulsa, Oklahoma. Edited by Harold K. Straughn.

Introduction

Life is filled with many puzzling questions and discouraging situations. However, God's Word, the Bible, has all the answers and encouragement we need. The Bible contains promises that apply to every area of our lives. There are promises dealing with everything from emotions and trials to relationships and finances.

God's Little Lessons for Dads gives you easy access to some of your most-needed answers. This conveniently sized book not only provides you with scriptures covering a multitude of topics, but it illustrates those topics with inspiring stories about dads and their children.

Just as Jesus taught in parables in order to bring divine mysteries to light, the devotional stories in *God's Little Lessons for Dads* will help you to grasp the reality of the Scriptures.

The promises of God are for you and your family. He is always ready and willing to bring them to fulfillment in your life. This book is designed to make you aware of His promises, so you can trust in His desire to take care of you.

Table of Contents

GOD's Little Lessons for Dads concerning:

Anger

A man of quick temper acts foolishly, but a man of discretion is patient.

Proverbs 14:17 RSV

The patient in spirit is better than the proud in spirit. Be not quick to anger, for anger lodges in the bosom of fools.

Ecclesiastes 7:8-9 RSV

How great a forest is set ablaze by a small fire! And the tongue is a fire.

James 3:5-6 NRSV

Since an overseer is entrusted with God's work, he must be blameless—not overbearing, not quick-tempered.

Titus 1:7

Eating Crow for Supper

One morning during the usual rush to get the family off to work and school, a father lost his temper and lashed out at his daughter, who just happened to be the closest target. Later that day, when the family was eating supper, Dad tried to make things right.

He began slowly. "I have something I want to talk to you about," he said, looking at everyone, but especially eyeing his daughter. "You all know how fast we rush around each morning."

"Uh . . . right," said his daughter.

"Well, I realize I was a little hard to be around this morning," he continued.

Silence.

"I . . . uh . . . want you all to know that I feel bad about it," he said. "And especially, Jane, I'm sorry for what I said to you this morning."

Finally his daughter spoke.

"Dad," she began, "I want you to know you teach me a lot of things, and I appreciate it."

"Just now," she said, and her face broke into a smile, "you are teaching me patience."

Our families have a way of "nailing us" with their honesty. Rather than being defensive, we should accept what they say and let it help us to grow into the image of Jesus Christ.

Anger

You must understand this, my beloved: let everyone be quick to listen, slow to speak, slow to anger.

James 1:19 NRSV

A soft answer turns away wrath, but a harsh word stirs up anger.

Proverbs 15:1 RSV

Good sense makes a man slow to anger, and it is his glory to overlook an offense.

Proverbs 19:11 RSV

Fathers, do not provoke your children to anger, but bring them up in the discipline and instruction of the Lord.

Ephesians 6:4 NRSV

How to Find a Lost Temper

Once a little boy suddenly became frustrated and screamed at his parents, *"I hate you! I hate you!"*

His father, instead of losing his own temper, asked his son to put on his coat. Together they walked to a nearby park where a stream had cut a deep valley into the hillside. There the father told the boy to yell just as he had inside the house.

"I hate you! I hate you!" shouted the boy. *"I hate you! I hate you!"* echoed the valley.

Startled, the boy looked at his father and whimpered, "Somebody down there doesn't like me."

"Maybe so," the father replied. "But see what happens when you tell them you love them."

The little boy did so, and this time he heard a voice replying, *"I love you! I love you!"*

Gazing at his dad in wide-eyed surprise, he stammered, "Look! I made a friend down there."

When we're able to deflect our children's anger with calmness, we can "teach them a lesson," all right—a lesson in self-control that will last far longer than any scolding or answering in kind.

As the ancient Roman sage, Seneca, reminds us, *"The greatest cure for anger is delay."*

Authority

You know that among the Gentiles those whom
they recognize as their rulers lord it over them,
and their great ones are tyrants over them. But it
is not so among you; but whoever wishes to
become great among you must be your servant.

Mark 10:42-43 NRSV

When you are invited by any one to a marriage
feast, do not sit down in a place of honor, lest a
more eminent man than you be invited by him;
and he who invited you both will come and say to
you, "Give place to this man," and then you will
begin with shame to take the lowest place.

Luke 14:8-9 RSV

Let the same mind be in you that was in Christ
Jesus, who, though he was in the form of God,
did not regard equality with God as something to
be exploited, but emptied himself, taking the form
of a slave, being born in human likeness.

Philippians 2:5-7 NRSV

A Roar Needs More

The lion was proud of his mastery of the jungle. One day he decided to remind all the animals who was king.

First he went to the bear and demanded, "Who is the king of the jungle?" The bear replied, "Why, you are, of course." The lion roared his approval.

Next he asked the tiger, "Who is the king of the jungle?" The tiger responded, "Everyone knows that you are, O mighty lion."

Then the lion bounded up to an elephant and started to ask the same question. Before he could even finish, the elephant grabbed the lion in his trunk, whirled him around and around in the air, and slammed him into a tree. Then he stomped on him several times, and finally dragged him to a river and tossed him in.

Battered, bruised, and bedraggled, the lion struggled onto dry land.

"Look," he said to the elephant, "just because you don't know the answer is no reason to get so sore about it."

Authority is more than mere company rank, or the power to coerce. Authority is the ability to command respect, and, like Christ, to inspire others to follow you because they trust you, rather than fear you.

Authority

When justice rules a nation, everyone is glad;
when injustice rules, everyone groans.

Proverbs 29:2 CEV

Gideon said to them, "I will not rule over you,
nor shall my son rule over you; the LORD shall
rules over you."

Judges 8:23 NASB

Let your light so shine before men, that they may
see your good works, and glorify your Father
which is in heaven.

Matthew 5:16 KJV

God did not give us a spirit of timidity, but a spirit
of power, of love and of self-discipline.

2 Timothy 1:7

A Steady Hand at the Wheel

On January 1, 1863, Abraham Lincoln spent the entire morning meeting dignitaries, shaking their hands, and spreading goodwill. Tired from his nonstop morning, Lincoln returned to his office at noon.

When he arrived, waiting in his office was the secretary of state, William Seward. He handed the president the final draft of the Emancipation Proclamation for his signature. Twice he picked up his pen to sign it, but his arm was so tired his hand shook.

President Lincoln turned to Seward and said, "I've been shaking hands since nine this morning, and I don't want to sign this document till my hand is more steady. If my name ever goes into history it will be for this act, and I know that my whole soul is in it. You see, if my hand trembles when I sign this proclamation, some will say, "He hesitated—look at his handwriting."

A short time later, the president took up his pen with a strong and steady hand and firmly wrote, "Abraham Lincoln." That historic act endeared him to the world as the Great Emancipator.

Ultimately, authority is a matter of character. Lincoln's character enabled him to see the lasting value of this apparently small act. As fathers, our character endures through the small acts we devote to our children.

Burdens

Cast your burden on the Lord, and he will sustain you.

Psalm 55:22 RSV

Come to me, all you who are weary and are carrying heavy burdens, and I will give you rest. Take my yoke upon you, and learn from me; for I am gentle and humble in heart, and you will find rest for your souls. For my yoke is easy, and my burden is light.

Matthew 11:28-30 NRSV

Do not do as they do, for they do not practice what they teach. They tie up heavy burdens, hard to bear, and lay them on the shoulders of others; but they themselves are unwilling to lift a finger to move them.

Matthew 23:3,4 NRSV

Carry each other's burdens, and in this way you will fulfill the law of Christ.

Galatians 6:2

Mr. Wonderful, That's You

Several years ago in the Paris opera house, a famous singer was scheduled to perform, and ticket sales were booming. The night of the concert was a sellout. A rush of excitement and anticipation filled the air as the house manager came to the microphone.

"Ladies and gentlemen, I am sorry I have bad news," he began. "I regret that the singer you've all come to hear will not be performing tonight due to illness. However, I am pleased to present in his absence a young and talented artist who will provide you with a fine evening's entertainment."

The audience groaned in disappointment, and sat back to endure the substitute soloist. The stand-in performer gave everything he had, but there was no comparing him with the marquee singer. When he had finished, there was only an uncomfortable silence.

Suddenly, from the balcony, a little boy stood up and shouted, "Daddy, I think you are wonderful!"

The crowd broke into thunderous applause.

Sometimes when we come home from a grueling and bruising day at work, all we may need is a smile from our child, and suddenly our burdens are miraculously lifted. Everybody needs to be "wonderful" in somebody's eyes.

Burdens

To grant to those who mourn in Zion—to give them a garland instead of ashes, the oil of gladness instead of mourning, the mantle of praise instead of a faint spirit; that they may be called oaks of righteousness, the planting of the Lord, that he may be glorified.

Isaiah 61:3 RSV

Sovereign LORD, you have made the heavens and the earth by your great power and outstretched arm. Nothing is too hard for you.

Jeremiah 32:17

These little troubles are getting us ready for an eternal glory that will make all our troubles seem like nothing.

2 Corinthians 4:17 CEV

Since I know it is all for Christ's good, I am quite content with my weaknesses and with insults, hardships, persecutions, and calamities. For when I am weak, then I am strong.

2 Corinthians 12:10 NLT

Lifting a Burden with a Finger

The Brooklyn Bridge that connects Manhattan
and Brooklyn was one of the wonders of the
world when it was finished in 1883. Yet it might
not have been built were it not for the devotion
between a father and his son.

A creative engineer named John Roebling came
up with the idea for the unique design, and he put
his young son Washington in charge of building
it. Only a few months into the project, however, a
tragic accident took the life of John Roebling and
severely injured Washington, who was left unable
to walk or talk. It seemed the bridge never would
be built, for the Roeblings were the only ones
who knew how to do it.

The son's desire to complete the bridge as a
tribute to his father drove him with heroic
determination. Confined to his hospital bed, he
developed a code. With the one finger he could
move he touched his wife's arm, tapping out
messages to the construction crew leaders. For the
next thirteen years he communicated his father's
vision until it became a spectacular reality.

For Washington Roebling, a driving dream
possessed the power to lift a heavy burden. Your
dream can do the same.

Children

These words which I command you this day shall
be upon your heart; and you shall teach them
diligently to your children.

Deuteronomy 6:6-7 RSV

Whoever welcomes a little child like this in my
name welcomes me.

Matthew 18:5

If anyone causes one of these little ones who
believe in me to sin, it would be better for him to
be thrown into the sea with a large millstone
around his neck.

Mark 9:42

Children ought not to lay up for their parents, but
parents for their children. I will most gladly spend
and be spent for you.

2 Corinthians 12:14-15
NRSV

The Fruits of Faith

Karl, a young Jewish boy in Germany, had a profound sense of admiration for his father. The life of the family centered on the prayers and acts of devotion prescribed by their faith.

When Karl was a teenager, the family moved to a new town. To Karl's surprise, his father announced to the family that they were going to abandon their Jewish traditions and join the Lutheran church. He explained that this was necessary to help his business, since the leading citizens of the town were Lutheran.

Karl was disappointed and confused by this action. His bewilderment gave way to anger and eventually, an intense bitterness. A few years later he left Germany and went to England to study. While there, he wrote an angry manuscript in which he termed religion an "opiate for the masses," and conceived of a movement that would change the world based on establishing a society on strictly economic terms.

Billions of people eventually came to live in this world. For that young man was Karl Marx, the founder of communism.

Your children are always aware of the depth and intensity of your beliefs. The fruit your children see in your life—good or bad—will produce a harvest in theirs.

Children

What pleasure a wise son is! So give your parents joy!

Proverbs 23:25 TLB

Whoever humbles himself like this child is the greatest in the kingdom of heaven.

Matthew 18:4

His disciples asked him, "Rabbi, who sinned, this man or his parents, that he was born blind?" "Neither this man nor his parents sinned," said Jesus, "but this happened so that the work of God might be displayed in his life."

John 9:2-3

I have no greater joy than this, to hear that my children are walking in the truth.

3 John 1:4 NRSV

Being Happy Is a Talent

Political commentator George F. Will has written lovingly about his son:

"Jon Frederick Will, the oldest of my four children, recently turned twenty-one, and on his birthday, as he does on every workday, he commuted by subway to his job delivering mail and being useful in other ways at the National Institute of Health. That my son is striding into a productive manhood with a spring in his step and Baltimore Orioles on his mind could not have been confidently predicted when he was born. . . .

"Jon has Down's syndrome. At the instant he was conceived, he lost one of life's lotteries, but he also was lucky: his physical abnormalities do not impede his vitality, and his mental retardation does not interfere with life's essential joys—receiving love, returning it, and reading baseball box scores.

"So one must mind one's language when speaking of people like Jon. He does not 'suffer from' Down's syndrome. It is an affliction, but he is happy. Happiness, in fact, is a talent, for which Jon has a superior aptitude."

Yes, "happiness is a talent." Every day we can increase our own happiness when we realize how much happiness can be found in spending time with our children.

Comfort

I will pray the Father, and he shall give you
another Comforter, that he may abide with you
for ever.

John 14:16 KJV

Your Father knows what you need before you
ask him.

Matthew 6:8

Even when walking through the dark valley of
death I will not be afraid, for you are close beside
me, guarding, guiding all the way.

Psalm 23:4 TLB

Where is God my Maker who gives songs in the
night?

Job 35:10 TLB

Your Father Knows the Way

A recollection by pastor-author James S. Hewitt:

When I was a small boy growing up in Pennsylvania, often we would visit my grandparents who lived nine miles away. One night a thick fog settled over the hilly countryside before we started home. I remember being terrified and asking if we shouldn't be going slower than we were. Mother said gently, "Don't worry. Your father knows the way."

You see, my dad had walked that road when there was no gasoline during the war. He had ridden that blacktop on his bicycle to court Mother. And for years he had made those weekly trips back to visit his own parents.

How often when I can't see the road ahead, and that feeling of being lost has returned, I hear the echo of my mother's voice: "Don't worry. Your father knows the way."

You never know when something you say or do might offer great comfort to your child. Often it's something offhand that you don't even remember. Simply being there is often the most effective way of teaching a child about the love and care of the Heavenly Father. Resolve today that you'll be there during the storms of their lives.

Comfort

Out of the mouth of babes and sucklings hast thou ordained strength.

Psalm 8:2 KJV

In that day... calves and fat cattle will be safe among lions, and a little child shall lead them all.

Isaiah 11:6 TLB

Better a poor but wise youth than an old but foolish king.

Ecclesiastes 4:13

Blessed be the God and Father of our Lord Jesus Christ, the Father of mercies and God of all comfort, who comforts us in all our tribulation, that we may be able to comfort those who are in any trouble.

2 Corinthians 1:3-4 NKJV

Comfort from Your Children

When pitcher Dave Dravecky first noticed the lump on his pitching arm, he had it checked out, but nothing seemed amiss. The lump continued to grow, however, and eventually he had it biopsied. The result came back: a cancer called fibrosarcoma. The treatment called for an aggressive surgery. Physicians held out little hope Dravecky would ever pitch again.

Dave and his wife Janice decided to tell their children, Tiffany and Jonathan, what was happening. As they tucked them into bed one night, they gently explained that Daddy was going to be in the hospital for awhile, and that he probably wouldn't be able to play baseball anymore. They waited for the news to sink in, thinking it would devastate them. Tiffany, however, responded by saying, "You mean we won't have to move anymore? I can stay in my same school? We'll be here in Ohio near Grandma and Grandpa all the time? Jonathan chimed in, "Dad, you mean you'll be able to play football with me every day?"

More than anything else, their reaction helped Dave cope with what lay ahead. In his words, they "put it all into perspective." Bring your children into the important decisions of your life. They may help you see things in a bright new light!

Conflict

How good and pleasant it is when brothers live together in unity!

Psalm 133:1

It's harder to make amends with an offended friend than to capture a fortified city. Arguments separate friends like a gate locked with iron bars.

Proverbs 18:19 NLT

He will lead children and parents to love each other more, so that when I come, I won't bring doom to the land.

Malachi 4:6 CEV

If therefore you are presenting your offering at the altar, and there remember that your brother has something against you, leave your offering there before the altar, and go your way; first be reconciled to your brother, and then come and present your offering.

Matthew 5:23-24 NASB

Never Too Late

Stewart decided to visit his twenty-year-old son at college. He asked the young man what it had been like growing up with him as a father. "Well, Dad," he said, "I don't want to hurt your feelings, but you were never there."

"What do you mean?" Stewart asked. "I was home every evening. I never went anywhere!"

His son said, "I know, Dad, but if you were ever sad, I never knew it. You never seemed happy. I didn't know who you were. Most of the time," and here his voice began to crack, "I felt like I didn't have a father."

Stewart broke down and sobbed uncontrollably. "Can you believe it?" he said through his tears. "I was there, right in front of you, all that time, and yet you felt I was invisible."

He and his son decided to change things. They joined an outdoor club together. On a deep-sea fishing trip he told his son, "I'm so angry at myself—and what I really regret is that I've hurt you so much—not by doing something mean, but because I failed to let you get to know me."

"Dad, I forgive you."

It's never too late to become a dad to your child! Don't let the fear of facing conflict keep you from reaping the benefits of relationship.

Conflict

And the son said unto him, Father, I have sinned against heaven, and in thy sight, and am no more worthy to be called thy son. But the father said to his servants, Bring forth the best robe, and put it on him; and put a ring on his hand, and shoes on his feet.

Luke 15:21-22 KJV

Even when we were God's enemies, he made peace with us, because his Son died for us. Yet something even greater than friendship is ours. Now that we are at peace with God, we will be saved by his Son's life.

Romans 5:10 CEV

All this is from God, who reconciled us to himself through Christ and gave us the ministry of reconciliation: that God was reconciling the world to himself in Christ, not counting men's sins against them. And he has committed to us the message of reconciliation.

2 Corinthians 5:18-19

You must make allowance for each other's faults and forgive the person who offends you. Remember, the Lord forgave you, so you must forgive others.

Colossians 3:13 NLT

Never Too Late for a Child
To Find a Father

A successful, respected executive gave his son the best of everything—the best schools, a new sports car, even a management-track position in his company. Then one day, his son was arrested for embezzling funds from their firm.

All through his trial, the young man appeared proud, nonchalant, and unrepentant. Then the jury brought in the verdict: Guilty on all counts. The judge ordered him to stand. He arose, still somewhat cocky and indifferent. As he glanced around the courtroom, he noticed that his father too was standing. The young man stared at his father for a long time. He began to realize that this man, who once strode so confidently with his head and shoulders ramrod straight, now stood with his back stooped, his head bowed with sorrow.

His father was acknowledging that he was partly responsible for what his son had become. He was prepared to receive, as though it was for himself, his son's sentence from the judge.

At the sight of his father, bent and humiliated, the son began to weep bitterly, and for the first time showed remorse for his crime.

Although our children are ultimately responsible for their own behavior as adults, we are responsible to train them to make the right choices in life.

Courage

"Be strong and of good courage, do not fear or be in dread of them: for it is the LORD your God who goes with you; he will not fail you or forsake you."

Deuteronomy 31:6 RSV

Fear of man will prove to be a snare, but whoever trusts in the LORD is kept safe.

Proverbs 29:25

Christ gives me the strength to face anything.

Philippians 4:13 CEV

We say with confidence, "The Lord is my helper; I will not be afraid. What can man do to me?"

Hebrews 13:6

Courage Is Its Own Reward

When Frank arrived at the Pearly Gates, he found himself standing face to face with an impressive angelic being holding a clipboard. The angel told Frank he needed to get some "entry data."

"Frank," the angel said, "it would help if you could identify one experience on earth where you performed a courageous, unselfish deed."

Frank thought for a few seconds and then said, "Well, one day as I was walking, I came upon an old woman who was being attacked by motorcycle gang members. As they were smacking her around, I stepped up and pushed over one of the cycles—but only to distract them. Then I kicked one of them real hard on the shins, and pushed him into the others, and shouted for the lady to run for help. Then I hauled off and put my fist right into the biggest guy's stomach. I think the woman made it to safety."

"Wow," the angel replied. That's very impressive. Then, with pen poised on his clipboard, he asked, "When did this happen?"

Frank looked at his watch and replied, "Oh, two or three minutes ago."

As Aesop once said, it is easy to be brave from a safe distance.

Courage

"If we are thrown in to the blazing furnace, the God we serve is able to save us from it, and he will rescue us from your hand, O king. But even if he does not, we want you to know, O king, that we will not serve your gods or worship the image of gold you have set up."

Daniel 3:17-18

Don't get tired of helping others. You will be rewarded when the time is right, if you don't give up.

Galatians 6:9 CEV

The members of the council were amazed when the saw the boldness of Peter and John, for they could see that they were ordinary men who had had no special training. They also recognized them as men who had been with Jesus.

Acts 4:13 NLT

Wherefore seeing we also are compassed about with so great a cloud of witnesses, let us lay aside every weight, and the sin which doth so easily beset us, and let us run with patience the race that is set before us.

Hebrews 12:1 KJV

The Courage To Risk

To laugh is to risk appearing the fool.

To weep is to risk appearing sentimental.

To reach out to another is to risk involvement.

To expose your feelings is to risk revealing your inner self.

To place your dreams before the crowd is to risk loss.

To love is to risk not being loved in return.

To hope is to risk despair.

To try is to risk failure.

To live is to risk dying.

Not to risk is the greatest risk of all.

"The paradox of courage," G.K. Chesterton once wrote, "is that a person must be a little careless of life in order to survive." Today, if you're wondering if you should stick your neck out or keep your mouth shut, remember that the moment you stop fighting for what matters, you begin to die.

Discipline

It is pleasant to see dreams come true, but fools will not turn from evil to attain them.

Proverbs 13:19 NLT

Everyone will hate you because of me. But if you keep on being faithful right to the end, you will be saved.

Mark 13:13 CEV

"Now get up and stand on your feet. I have appeared to you to appoint you as a servant and as a witness of what you have seen of me and what I will show you."

Acts 26:16

Therefore, take up the full armor of God, that you may be able to resist in the evil day, and having done everything, to stand firm.

Ephesians 6:13 NASB

The Only Difference Between Mark Twain and Me

A scholar decided to write a biography of Mark Twain. After researching the basic facts about his life, the biographer traveled to Hannibal, Missouri, to visit sites made famous by the great storyteller.

He started by floating a raft down the Mississippi. He located the cave where Tom Sawyer and Becky Thatcher became lost and explored its furthest reaches. He visited the cemetery where Tom and Huckleberry Finn got the scare of their lives and identified the very fence Tom finagled his friends into whitewashing for him.

In spite of all the biographer learned, the essence of the great man remained elusive. He searched the town for anyone still alive who remembered Mark Twain. He found a group of grizzled old cronies at a bar where they gathered to reminisce about old times.

"Yep, I remember him," answered one fellow. "He was full of stories all right. But I knew as many tales as Sam Clemens did. The only difference is, he wrote 'em down."

Often the main difference between leaving a legacy and living in obscurity is not so much talent or knowledge as it is discipline. Give your child the precious legacy of an example of personal discipline.

Discipline

Give instruction to a wise man, and he will be still wiser; teach a righteous man and he will increase in learning.

Proverbs 9:9 RSV

And you have forgotten that word of encouragement that addresses you as sons: "My son, do not make light of the Lord's discipline, and do not lose heart when he rebukes you, because the Lord disciplines those he loves, and he punishes everyone he accepts as a son."

Hebrews 12:5-6

Everything in the Scriptures is God's Word. All of it is useful for teaching and helping people and for correcting them and showing them how to live.

2 Timothy 3:16 CEV

Preach the word of God. Be persistent, whether the time is favorable or not. Patiently correct, rebuke, and encourage your people with good teaching.

2 Timothy 4:2 NLT

How Discipline Builds Character

Young Ted sat in his backyard, listening to his father brag on him to a neighbor. His dad was proudly telling about a time when Ted scored the winning points in a close basketball game.

All the time his father was speaking, Ted kept tugging at his dad's pants leg. The father, getting more and more annoyed, finally snapped, "What do you want?" "Dad," the child replied, "I've been tryin' to tell you. You got it all wrong. It wasn't me in that game—it was Billy."

Embarrassed at the smirk his neighbor gave him, the father grabbed Ted and hauled him into the house. All the way there, Ted kept saying, "Dad! Dad!" "Now what?" his father said. I suppose you're going to tell me it was Billy, not you, who ridiculed me out there in front of my friend?"

"No," sobbed Ted. "I'm trying to say that tomorrow you can brag to your friend how you didn't punish me even when you wanted to."

As the saying goes, praise your children openly, but reprove them in secret. Discipline must be centered on building your child's character, not on expressing your own feelings.

Disappointment

Teach us to number our days aright, that we may gain a heart of wisdom.

Psalm 90:12

Do not boast about tomorrow, For you do not know what a day may bring forth.

Proverbs 27:1 NASB

Why waste your money on what really isn't food? Why work hard for something that doesn't satisfy? Listen carefully to me, and you will enjoy the very best foods.

Isaiah 55:2 CEV

It will be like a woman experiencing the pains of labor. When her child is born, her anguish gives place to joy because she has brought a new person into the world. You have sorrow now, but I will see you again; then you will rejoice, and no one can rob you of that joy.

John 16:21-22 NLT

Just Five More Minutes

A woman sat on a park bench next to a man looking out at the playground.

"That's my daughter," he said, pointing to a little girl who was gliding down the slide. Then, looking at his watch, he called to his daughter, "What do you say we go, Samantha?"

Samantha pleaded, "Just five minutes more, Dad. Please? Just five more minutes." The man nodded and she continued to play to her heart's content.

Minutes later he stood and called, "Time to go now." Again she pleaded, "Five more minutes, Dad, just five more minutes." Her dad smiled and said, "Okay."

"My, you certainly are a patient father," the woman responded.

"Last year," he said, "our son Tommy was killed by a drunk driver while riding his bike near here. I never spent much time with Tommy and now I'd give anything for just five more minutes with him. I vowed I wouldn't make the same mistake with Samantha. She thinks she has five more minutes to swing. Truth is, I get five more minutes with her."

There will be plenty of opportunity for your child to experience disappointment in life, without you being the cause of it. Next time you become impatient with your child, ask yourself: would you really be in such a rush if this were your child's last day on earth?

Disappointment

And the king was deeply moved and went up to the chamber over the gate and wept. And thus he said as he walked, "O my son Absalom, my son, my son Absalom! Would I had died instead of you, O Absalom, my son, my son!"

2 Samuel 18:33 NASB

We cried as we went out to plant our seeds. Now let us celebrate as we bring in the crops. We cried on the way to plant our seeds, but we will celebrate and shout as we bring in the crops.

Psalm 126:5-6 CEV

Your people will rebuild the ancient ruins and will raise up the age-old foundations; you will be called Repairer of Broken Walls, Restorer of Streets with Dwellings.

Isaiah 58:12

By him God reconciled everything to himself. He made peace with everything in heaven and on earth by means of his blood on the cross.

Colossians 1:20 NLT

From Disappointment to Dependability

During the Civil War, the son of a devout Quaker family ran off and enlisted in the army to the great disappointment of his peace-loving father.

One night the father had a dream that his son had been wounded in action and was calling out his name. Preparing his horse-drawn buggy, he rode for days to the scene of combat. He inquired of the commander where he might find his son. Sadly, the commander replied that many wounded remained on the battlefield after heavy action that day, but he gave the father permission to go in search of his son.

Making his way through the dreadful carnage, he called out his son's name: "Jonathan Smythe, thy father seeketh after thee."

Finally he heard a faint, barely audible cry, "Father, over here." Hurrying to the familiar voice he found his son, lying mortally wounded. As he cradled the boy in his arms, suddenly he opened his eyes, and said, "Hello father. I knew you'd come." And then he breathed his last.

Our disappointments tell us much about our expectations—and very little about our circumstances. The next time you're tempted to be disappointed in your child, remember how much that child is depending on you.

Encouragement

All the men of Israel were gathered against the city, knit together as one man.

Judges 20:11 KJV

Do not fear, for I am with you; Do not anxiously look about you, for I am your God. I will strengthen you, surely I will help you, Surely I will uphold you with My righteous right hand.

Isaiah 41:10 NASB

The LORD God gives me the right words to encourage the weary. Each morning he awakens me eager to learn his teaching.

Isaiah 50:4 CEV

Therefore each of you must put off falsehood and speak truthfully to his neighbor, for we are all members of one body.

Ephesians 4:25

Holding Your Team Together

The legendary Alabama football coach, Bear Bryant, was known as much for his principles of leadership as for his lifetime winning record. He understood the essential value of encouragement. He was a much-in-demand speaker, and millions paid large amounts just to hear him talk about his secrets of success. Bryant's speeches, however, were low-key and understated, delivered in a soft, slow drawl. They usually went something like this:

"I'm just a plowhand from Arkansas, but I have learned a few things about how to hold a team together.

"I've learned that some need lifting up, while others need calming down, until, finally, they've got one heartbeat together, and now they're a team.

"I can think of only three things I'd ever say about how to win:

"If anything goes bad, I did it.

"If anything goes semi-good, then we did it.

"If anything goes real good, then you did it.

"That's pretty much it. That's all it takes to get people to win football games for you."

Accepting your children is the way to show them you love them as they are. Encouraging your children is the way you help them believe in what they may yet become with God's help.

Encouragement

Wait for the LORD; be strong and take heart and wait for the LORD.

Psalm 27:14

But now, O Israel, the LORD who created you says: "Do not be afraid, for I have ransomed you. I have called you by name; you are mine. When you go through deep waters and great trouble, I will be with you. When you go through rivers of difficulty, you will not drown! When you walk through the fire of oppression, you will not be burned up; the flames will not consume you.

Isaiah 43:1-2 NLT

Remember the Lord's people who are in jail and be concerned for them. Don't forget those who are suffering, but imagine that you are there with them.

Hebrews 13:3 CEV

For you have been called for this purpose, since Christ also suffered for you, leaving you an example for you to follow in His steps.

1 Peter 2:21 NASB

An Encouraging Word

As a teenager, Daniel Webster left his home in the Massachusetts countryside to head to Boston to study law. No law schools existed in his day, therefore the custom was to apprentice to a practicing attorney.

Webster first went unannounced to the head of the state bar, Christopher Gore. He took his place among several young men competing for Mr. Gore's attention. But the poor, roughly dressed young Daniel was looked upon with contempt by his peers, and was scarcely acknowledged by anyone in the law firm.

Then one day the respected lawyer Rufus King approached him and asked his name. King smiled warmly and said, "I know your father well. He is a fine man, and you must be, too." Then he encouraged Daniel: "Be studious and you will win. I will keep an eye on you."

Years later, the great statesman recalled: "I can still feel the warm pressure of that hand and hear those challenging words of encouragement."

As a father, your reputation is one of the most valuable treasures you can pass along to your child. There's no way to measure how encouraging it can be for a child to hear someone say, "I know your father well."

Failure

"At least there is hope for a tree: If it is cut down,
it will sprout again, and its new shoots will not
fail. Its roots may grow old in the ground and its
stump die in the soil, yet at the scent of water it
will bud and put forth shoots like a plant."

Job 14:7-9

And the Lord said, Simon, Simon, behold, Satan
hath desired to have you, that he may sift you as
wheat: But I have prayed for thee, that thy faith
fail not: and when thou art converted, strengthen
thy brethren.

Luke 22:31-32 KJV

We can rejoice, too, when we run into problems
and trials, for we know that they are good for us—
they help us learn to endure. And endurance
develops strength of character in us, and character
strengthens our confident expectation of salvation.

Romans 5:3-4 NLT

We never give up. Our bodies are gradually dying,
but we ourselves are being made stronger each
day.

2 Corinthians 4:16 CEV

Top 10

Guess these Top Ten failures of all time:

10. The engineer who neglected to design a reverse gear in the first car he manufactured.

9. The group turned down by Decca Records because "guitars are on their way out."

8. The illustrator told by his newspaper editor to pursue another line of work.

7. The skinny kid who hated the way he looked and was always being beat up by bullies.

6. The seriously ill, deeply in debt composer who in desperation wrote an oratorio in a few hours.

5. The obese, bald, deformed eccentric who became a reclusive thinker.

4. The orchestra conductor-composer who made his greatest contributions after becoming deaf.

3. The politician who lost his first seven elections.

2. The boy everyone thought was mute because his stuttering was so bad he never spoke until he was a teenager.

1. The woman born deaf and blind who became a great writer and philanthropist, and once said, "I thank God for my handicaps."

Answers:
*10. Henry Ford. 9. The Beatles. 8. Walt Disney.
7. Charles Atlas. 6. George Frederick Handel* (The Messiah). *5. Socrates. 4. Ludwig von Beethoven.
3. Abraham Lincoln. 2. James Earl Jones. 1. Helen Keller.*

Our greatest failures can produce our greatest successes.

Failure

The righteous face many troubles, but the LORD
rescues them from each and every one.
Psalm 34:19 NLT

The Lord says, "If you love me and truly know
who I am, I will rescue you and keep you safe.
When you are in trouble, call out to me. I will
answer and be there to protect and honor you."
Psalm 91:14-15 CEV

These things I have spoken unto you, that in me
ye might have peace. In the world ye shall have
tribulation: but be of good cheer; I have overcome
the world.

John 16:33 KJV

Humble yourselves therefore under the mighty
hand of God, that in due time he may exalt you.
Cast all your anxieties on him, for he cares about
you.

1 Peter 5:6-7 RSV

The Flint That Lights Other People's Torches

Author Phyllis Theroux writes about how her father helped her deal with failure:

"If there was any one thing my father did for me when I was growing up it was to give me the promise that ahead of me was dry land—a bright, marshless territory, without chuckholes or traps, where one day I would walk easily and as befitting my talents. . . .

"Thus it was, when he came upon me one afternoon sobbing out my unsuccesses into a wet pillow, that he sat down on the bed and assured me that my grief was only a temporary setback. Oh, very temporary! Why, he couldn't think of any other little girl who was so talented, so predestined to succeed in every department as I was. 'And don't forget,' he added with a smile, 'that we can trace our ancestry right back to Pepin the Stupid!'

"There are some people who carry the flint that lights other people's torches. . . . That was my father's gift to me."

Today before the sun goes down, your child is likely to experience one of those "unsuccesses" that needs your simple, comforting words, "This, too, shall pass." Be watchful for the opportunity to give your child this unforgettable, invaluable experience.

Faith

O our God, wilt thou not judge them? for we have no might against this great company that cometh against us; neither know we what to do: but our eyes are upon thee.

2 Chronicles 20:12 KJV

Immediately the boy's father exclaimed, "I do believe; help me overcome my unbelief!"

Mark 9:24

The good news tells how God accepts everyone who has faith, but only those who have faith.

Romans 1:17 CEV

What is faith? It is the confident assurance that what we hope for is going to happen. It is the evidence of things we cannot yet see.

Hebrews 11:1 NLT

Frantic Faith

Bruce Larson tells this story about a test of his faith:

"A few years ago I almost drowned in a storm at sea in the Gulf of Mexico when I found myself swimming far from shore, having tried to retrieve my drifting boat. The waves were seven or eight feet high, and the sky was dark with gale force winds and lightning. I can remember saying, 'Well, this is it.'

"I was drifting out to sea when the word of the Lord came to me and saved my life. What I thought He said was, 'I'm here, Larson, and you're not coming home as soon as you think. Can you tread water?'

"Somehow that had never occurred to me. Had I continued my frantic effort to swim back to shore, I would have exhausted my strength and gone down.

"Too often we make matters worse by our frantic efforts to save ourselves when God is trying to tell us, 'Stand still.' We get ourselves into hopeless situations and the more we do the worse it gets."

The faith we want to pass to our children has been tempered by our own experience. Tell your children stories of *your* adventures in faith.

Faith

When I look at the night sky and see the work of you fingers—the moon and the stars you have set in place—what are mortals that you should think of us, mere humans that you should care for us? For you made us only a little lower than God, and you crowned us with glory and honor.

Psalm 8:3-5 NLT

Let love and faithfulness never leave you; bind them around your neck, write them on the tablet of your heart.

Proverbs 3:3

Every child of God can defeat the world, and our faith is what gives us this victory.

1 John 5:4 CEV

His master said to him, "Well done, good and faithful servant; you have been faithful over a little, I will set you over much; enter into the joy of your master."

Matthew 25:21 RSV

A Motto for Your Life

When Professor Charles William Eliot was
president of Harvard University, he had occasion
to dedicate a new hall of philosophy and searched
for an appropriate inscription to place above its
entrance.

He called together his faculty members and
after much deliberation they agreed upon the well-
known Greek maxim, "Man is the measure of all
things." With that they adjourned for summer
vacation.

When school reopened in the fall, they were
surprised to find that the president had decided
upon his own inscription. Instead of the human-
centered "Man is the measure of all things," he
had seen fit to inscribe the prayerful words of the
biblical psalm, "What is man that Thou art
mindful of him?"

Suppose you were to choose a motto for your
life. What words might you choose? Would they
express your goals or dreams or achievements, or
would they point others to the Source of all these
things? You may never be asked to carve an
inscription over the threshold of a great building,
but even today you can place thoughtful
quotations on a bulletin board where you work to
encourage your co-workers. Or put them on the
refrigerator door at home in order to teach your
children the elements of your faith.

Family

"I will be a Father to you, and you will be my sons and daughters, says the Lord Almighty."
2 Corinthians 6:18

"Obey your father and your mother, and you will have a long and happy life."
Ephesians 6:2-3 CEV

But if any provide not for his own, and specially for those of his own house, he hath denied the faith, and is worse than an infidel.
1 Timothy 5:8 KJV

So then, while we have opportunity, let us do good to all men, and especially to those who are of the household of the faith.
Galatians 6:10 NASB

Qualities of a Healthy Family

Andy Rooney, the philosopher-in-residence of "Sixty Minutes," offers this description of the kind of family it takes to bring up a responsible and productive member of society:

- A home with one mother and one father.
- A family that eats dinner together.
- A space of their own, even if it's tiny.
- A good night kiss.
- A warm bed with a special blanket or quilt with its own character.
- A sweet, motherly kindergarten teacher.
- A cake on every birthday with candles to blow out with a wish.
- A place to swim, and a place to sleigh-ride.
- A friend with whom to share secrets.
- Some minor illnesses to let the child know life isn't always a bowl of cherries.
- A rich uncle or doting aunt.
- Talent that parents encourage—because every child is good at something.
- Discipline.
- Someone who will read them stories.

Parenting sometimes seems like such a monumental task, but as you look over this list, you can see that these are all pretty simple things. How many of these fourteen qualities are well developed in your family? Which one needs a bit of improvement that you can start to work on today?

Family

Better a meal of vegetables where there is love than a fattened calf with hatred.

Proverbs 15:17

Don't be cruel to any of these little ones! I promise you that their angels are always with my Father in heaven.

Matthew 18:10-11 CEV

I have written unto you, fathers, because ye have known him that is from the beginning. I have written unto you, young men, because ye are strong, and the word of God abideth in you, and ye have overcome the wicked one.

1 John 2:14 KJV

See how very much our heavenly Father loves us, for he allows us to be called his children, and we really are! But the people who belong to this world don't know God, so they don't understand that we are his children.

1 John 3:1 NLT

What's in Your Wallet?

Two tough young kids hanging out on their
accustomed corner noticed that every night at
6:30, a certain man passed by. He always carried a
lunch pail in one hand and a couple of bags of
groceries in the other. They also noticed a bulging
wallet in the hip pocket of his work pants.

One night they devised a plan to mug him. Sure
enough, right at 6:30 here he came. Quickly they
ambushed him, one in front and one behind.
Knocking the groceries to the sidewalk, they
tossed away his lunch pail, slammed him against
the wall, and grabbed his fat wallet.

Leaving him bloodied and dazed, groceries
scattered everywhere, the thugs raced away, not
stopping till they rounded the corner into a dark
alley. "All right!" they congratulated themselves
with high fives. "Let's see how much we got."

Shaking everything out on the ground, their
eyes grew wide as they surveyed the contents.

Two one-dollar bills. And two long foldouts of
picture after picture of the man's six children.

If somebody were to look through the contents
of your wallet, what evidence would they find of
your love for your family? What kind of treasure
do you carry in your wallet?

Fear

I sought the LORD, and he answered me; he delivered me from all my fears.

Psalm 34:4

I trust you to save me, LORD God, and I won't be afraid. My power and my strength come from you, and you have saved me.

Isaiah 12:2 CEV

For God has not given us a spirit of fear and timidity, but of power, love, and self-discipline.

2 Timothy 1:7 NLT

There is no fear in love, but perfect love casts out fear. For fear has to do with punishment, and he who fears is not perfected in love.

1 John 4:18 RSV

Praying for Snakes

A widowed farmer tried to raise his three sons, Jim, John, and Sam, by himself. No one in the family ever attended church or thought much about God. Then one day a rattlesnake bit young Sam. The doctor quickly arrived, but the outlook for recovery looked very dim. At last the local minister was called and asked to come and pray.

The preacher arrived by Sam's beside, and this is what he said:

"O Lord, we thank Thee that Thou has sent this rattlesnake to bite Sam. It is doubtful that he has, in his brief life, ever prayed or even acknowledged Thine existence. We pray that this experience will lead him to healing and to a changed life.

"We also pray, O Lord, that Thou wilt send another rattlesnake to bite Jim, and another to bite John, and another really big one to bite the old man. For it seems that the efforts of all Thy servants around here have been in vain, for what we could not do this rattlesnake has done.

"So Lord, send us bigger and better rattlesnakes. Amen."

Fathers who nurture their children appropriately need apply fear only as a last resort.

Fear

God is our refuge and strength, A very present help in trouble. Therefore we will not fear, though the earth should change, And though the mountains slip into the heart of the sea.

Psalm 46:1-2 NASB

My slanderers pursue me all day long; many are attacking me in their pride. When I am afraid, I will trust in you. In God, whose word I praise, in God I trust; I will not be afraid. What can mortal man do to me?

Psalm 56:2-4

That he would grant unto us, that we being delivered out of the hand of our enemies might serve him without fear.

Luke 1:74 KJV

Be glad for the chance to suffer as Christ suffered. It will prepare you for even greater happiness when he makes his glorious return. Count it a blessing when you suffer for being a Christian. This shows that God's glorious Spirit is with you.

1 Peter 4:13-14 CEV

Tigers in the Dark

One night at a circus that drew a packed
audience of children and their parents, the tiger
trainer came out to perform. After bowing to loud
applause, he went into the cage. A hush drifted
over the audience as the door was locked behind
him.

Suddenly, as the trainer skillfully put the tigers
through their paces, everyone heard a loud *Pop!*
followed by the complete blackout of a power
failure. For several long minutes the trainer was
locked in the dark with the tigers, knowing they
could see him with their powerful night vision,
but he could not see them. A whip and a small
kitchen chair seemed meager protection.

Finally the lights came back on, and the trainer
finished his performance. Later, in a TV interview,
he admitted his first chilling fears. Then he
realized that the tigers *did not know* he could not
see them. "I just cracked my whip and talked to
them," he said, "until the lights came on."

At some point in life everyone will confront the
terror of tigers in the dark. The assurance we can
give our kids is that with God's help, our terrors
never will be able to exploit their temporary
advantage over us.

Finances

"Two things I ask of you, O LORD; do not refuse me before I die: Keep falsehood and lies far from me; give me neither poverty nor riches, but give me only my daily bread. Otherwise, I may have too much and disown you and say, 'Who is the LORD?' Or I may become poor and steal, and so dishonor the name of my God."

Proverbs 30:7-9

If you are thirsty, come and drink water! If you don't have any money, come, eat what you want! Drink wine and milk without paying a cent. Why waste your money on what really isn't food? Why work hard for something that doesn't satisfy? Listen carefully to me, and you will enjoy the very best foods.

Isaiah 55:1-2 CEV

He that loveth silver shall not be satisfied with silver; nor he that loveth abundance with increase: This is also vanity.

Ecclesiastes 5:10 KJV

He will give you all you need from day to day if you live for him and make the Kingdom of God your primary concern.

Matthew 6:33 NLT

What Would Jesus Drive?

On his sixteenth birthday, Danny and his father had their important heart-to-heart talk about cars. "When can I drive the family car?" Danny wanted to know.

"Son," his father began, "driving a car costs money and takes maturity. I want you to show me you're up to it. First, I want you to improve your grades. Second, I want you to read your Bible every day. And finally, I want you to get a haircut."

So Danny began the task of fulfilling his father's requirements. Next time grade reports came out, Danny came to his dad with a big smile, and said, "Look, Dad, all A's and B's. Now can I drive?"

"Great, son," his father said. You're one-third of the way there. Have you been reading the Bible daily?"

"Yes," Danny replied.

"Fine. You're two-thirds there. Now, when are you going to get that haircut?"

Danny frowned and said, "I don't see what a haircut has to do with driving. Jesus had long hair, right?"

"True," his dad replied. "And Jesus walked everywhere he went."

Getting through important passages in a child's life can bring tension and conflict, especially when it involves money; or it can be a time of fun and increased closeness. Humor really helps.

Finances

When you give to someone, don't tell your left hand what your right hand is doing. Give your gifts in secret, and your Father, who knows all secrets, will reward you.

Matthew 6:3-4 NLT

"Do not store up for yourselves treasures on earth, where moth and rust destroy, and where thieves break in and steal. But store up for yourselves treasures in heaven, where moth and rust do not destroy, and where thieves do not break in and steal."

Matthew 6:19-20

Therefore all things whatsoever ye would that men should do to you, do ye even so to them: for this is the law and the prophets.

Matthew 7:12 KJV

For we brought nothing into the world, and we cannot take anything out of the world.

1 Timothy 6:7 RSV

Whoever Has the Gold Makes the Rules

In Seoul, Korea, a wealthy visiting American textile executive was the after-dinner speaker for a large organization of Korean business leaders. To get his audience in a positive mood, the speaker told what he thought was a funny but long and rather rambling story then waited for the translator to relay it to his listeners.

After only a few words, the audience laughed uproariously and applauded at length. The speaker was so surprised he was barely able to complete his address. As soon as he was finished, he headed straight for the translator and complimented him for his efforts.

"I especially appreciate the way you translated my joke," he said. "I think it's wonderful that you helped me make such a good impression—and especially how you were able to shorten it in Korean."

"Think nothing of it," the interpreter replied. "I merely said, 'Man with big checkbook has told funny story. Do what you think is appropriate.'"

Our lore is packed with stories that illustrate, humorously or not, the fact that too often our society has inverted the Golden Rule to read: Whoever has the gold makes the rules. What values do your children pick up when they observe your attitude toward money?

Forgiveness

So if you are about to place your gift on the altar
and remember that someone is angry with you,
leave your gift there in front of the altar. Make
peace with that person, then come back and offer
your gift to God.

Matthew 5:23-24 CEV

Then Peter came and said to Him, "Lord, how
often shall my brother sin against me and I forgive
him? Up to seven times?" Jesus said to him, "I do
not say to you, up to seven times, but up to
seventy times seven."

Matthew 18:21-22 NASB

"Therefore, I tell you, her many sins have been
forgiven—for she loved much. But he who has
been forgiven little loves little."

Luke 7:47

And forgive us our sins; for we also forgive every
one that is indebted to us. And lead us not into
temptation; but deliver us from evil.

Luke 11:4 KJV

Forgiveness Lasts Forever

As a young, struggling attorney, Abraham Lincoln got a chance to work with some famous big-city defense lawyers on a local case. One of the outsiders, upon seeing Lincoln, gasped, "What is that gawky ape doing here? Get him out of here. I refuse to work with him."

Lincoln pretended not to hear, and continued to work with the legal team, even though they ostracized him and rarely consulted him. Observing the insulting but talented lawyer at work, however, Lincoln was so impressed by his skills that he decided to return to the study of law to improve himself.

Years later, after Lincoln became president, the offensive lawyer, now a U.S. senator, was one of his most outspoken critics. Yet, when the need arose for a knowledgeable secretary of war, Lincoln chose this man, Edwin M. Stanton.

Not long afterward, an assassin's bullet fatally pierced Lincoln's body. Stanton, filled with inconsolable grief, cried out the now-famous words, "Now he belongs to the ages!"

Lincoln may never have known the impact of his forgiving spirit upon this lifelong critic, but both men were ennobled because he chose to emphasize Stanton's positive qualities and to look beyond his negative ones.

Forgiveness

You are forgiving and good, O Lord, abounding in love to all who call to you.

Psalm 86:5

"Come now, let us reason together, says the LORD: though your sins are like scarlet, they shall be as white as snow; though they are red like crimson, they shall become like wool."

Isaiah 1:18 RSV

Our God, no one is like you. We are all that is left of your chosen people, and you freely forgive our sin and guilt. You don't stay angry forever; you're glad to have pity.

Micah 7:18 CEV

Dear brothers and sisters, if another Christian is overcome by some sin, you who are godly should gently and humbly help that person back onto the right path. And be careful not to fall into the same temptation yourself.

Galatians 6:1 NLT

Fishing for Sins

A young boy and his dad were returning home from a shopping mall, and the boy had acted badly—running off, being uncooperative, wanting this and that, etc. He could tell his father was in a bad mood, and he tried to broach the subject of his behavior.

"When we ask God to forgive us when we are bad," he asked, "He does, doesn't He?"

"Yes, He does," his father replied.

"And when He forgives us, He doesn't remember them anymore, right?" the son asked.

"That's right," said his father, growing more charitable. "It's like the song we sing at church, that God buries our sins in the deepest sea."

The boy was silent for awhile. Then he said, "I've asked God to forgive me, and now I want to ask you to promise me something."

"What's that, son?" said his father, pleased at this display of contrition.

"I want you to promise that when we get home you won't go fishing for those sins, okay?"

Most dads can identify with the impression this child has received from his father. One of the most important lessons we can teach by example is that forgiven sins stay forgiven—no fishing allowed.

Friendship

After David had finished talking with Saul, he met Jonathan, the king's son. There was an immediate bond of love between them, and they became the best of friends.

1 Samuel 18:1 NLT

A friend is always a friend, and relatives are born to share our troubles.

Proverbs 17:17 CEV

Two are better than one; because they have a good reward for their labour. For if they fall, the one will lift up his fellow: but woe to him that is alone when he falleth; for he hath not another to help him up.

Ecclesiastes 4:9-10 KJV

Greater love has no man than this, that a man lay down his life for his friends.

John 15:13 RSV

Even Heroes Need a Friend

Babe Ruth was one of baseball's immortals. The 1998 feats by Mark McGuire and Sammy Sosa remind us of that other time when fans packed stadiums to glimpse a hero who played for the other side.

As the Babe grew older, he continued to play, for he earned no rich pensions or fat commercial contracts. Finally, the Yankees traded Ruth to the lowly Boston Braves.

His final year, he had one nightmarish game. He struck out several times. He made several errors, and in one inning allowed five unearned runs to score.

Fans began to boo. "Hang it up!" they shouted. "You're a has-been!" When the horrible inning finally ended, Babe Ruth stumbled toward the dugout, hanging his head.

Suddenly a young boy jumped over the railing and with tears streaming down his cheeks ran out to the great athlete and flung his arms around one leg. The Babe reached down and scooped him up in his arms. Instantly the crowd hushed, and in awed silence watched as the Babe and the boy made their way to the dugout.

Sometimes the world can turn suddenly cruel, but all it takes to change everything is a simple gesture from a friend.

Friendship

I no longer call you servants, because a master doesn't confide in his servants. Now you are my friends, since I have told you everything the Father told me.

John 15:15 NLT

Be not forgetful to entertain strangers: for thereby some have entertained angels unawares.

Hebrews 13:2 KJV

This is what the Scriptures mean by saying, "Abraham had faith in God, and God was pleased with him." That's how Abraham became God's friend.

James 2:23 CEV

"Behold, I stand at the door and knock; if anyone hears My voice and opens the door, I will come in to him, and will dine with him, and he with Me."

Revelation 3:20 NASB

Friends Don't Let Friends Eat Alone

Here's a great place to find some words that are friendly and warm—the story of Winnie the Pooh.

One day Winnie the Pooh decide to go for a walk in the Hundred-Acre Wood. It's about 11:30 in the morning, just before lunch—a fine time to go walking.

Pooh sets off across the stream, stepping on the stones, and when he gets right in the middle of the stream, he sits down on a warm rock and thinks about which of his friends would be the best one to visit.

"I think I'll go see Tigger," he says to himself. Then he remembers that Tigger is in a bad mood.

"Owl," he thinks. Then, "No, Owl uses big words, hard-to-understand words."

At last, he brightens up.

"I know! I think I'll go see Rabbit. I like Rabbit. Rabbit uses encouraging words like, 'How's about lunch?' and 'Help yourself to some more, Pooh!' Yes, I think I'll go see Rabbit."

What a charming story about friendship! Reading stories is a magical way to deepen your friendship with your child. You can be sure that a question will come up, or a thought or a feeling, that offers you a special teaching moment.

Gentleness

But the meek will inherit the land and enjoy great peace.

Psalm 37:11

The LORD God has told us what is right and what he demands: "See that justice is done, let mercy be your first concern, and humbly obey your God."

Micah 6:8 CEV

And be kind to one another, tender-hearted, forgiving each other, just as God in Christ also has forgiven you.

Ephesians 4:32 NASB

But the wisdom that comes from heaven is first of all pure. It is also peace loving, gentle at all times, and willing to yield to others. It is full of mercy and good deeds. It shows no partiality and is always sincere.

James 3:17 NLT

The Greatness of Gentleness

During the Civil War, Abraham Lincoln often visited the hospitals to comfort the wounded. On one occasion, he approached the bedside of a young soldier who was very near death.

"Is there anything I can do for you?" asked the president. Not recognizing the famous face through his pain, the dying man struggled to speak.

"Would you please write a letter to my mother?" he whispered. Finding paper and pen, Lincoln carefully wrote each word the youth dictated:

"My dearest Mother, I was badly hurt while doing my duty. I'm afraid I am not going to recover. Don't grieve too much for me, please. Kiss Mary and John for me. May God bless you and father."

The young man was too weak to go on, so Lincoln signed the letter for him, and then added this postscript: "Written for your son by Abraham Lincoln."

Asking to see the note, the soldier smiled to discover who had treated him with such kindness. Then taking the lad's hand, Lincoln stayed until death overtook him with the dawn.

The man charged with leading an army, then binding a nation's wounds, also saw it as his duty to attend a dying soldier. Such is the nature of a gentle spirit.

Gentleness

The Lord is good to all: and his tender mercies are over all his works.

Psalm 145:9 KJV

He will feed his flock like a shepherd, he will gather the lambs in his arms, he will carry them in his bosom, and gently lead those that are with young.

Isaiah 40:11 RSV

Don't be troubled. You trust God, now trust in me. There are many rooms in my Father's home, and I am going to prepare a place for you. If this were not so, I would tell you plainly. When everything is ready, I will come and get you, so that you will always be with me where I am.

John 14:1-3 NLT

Christ encourages you, and his love comforts you. God's Spirit unites you, and you are concerned for others. Now make me completely happy! Live in harmony by showing love for each other. Be united in what you think, as if you were only one person.

Philippians 2:1-2 CEV

The Life-Giving Power of Gentleness

A doctor in the children's unit of a large
Southern California hospital conducted a visiting
group through the ward. All during the tour, the
group could hear the searing cry of a baby coming
from one of the rooms.

Finally the group arrived at the room. There lay
a child about a year old. She was covered with
terrible scars, bruises, and sores from head to toe.

The doctor explained that the little girl was the
victim of terrible abuse. Her internal injuries were
so severe that she couldn't keep food down.
Cigarette burns scarred the soles of her feet.
Obscenities were written in ink on her legs.

The doctor then leaned over the crib and very
gently and carefully lifted the child and held it
close. At first the child screamed all the more, as if
suspicious of every touch. But as the doctor held
the little girl, not tightly, but securely, she slowly
began to quiet down. In a few moments, she fell
asleep in the doctor's arms.

Sometimes our efforts to help others, like those
of the doctor, may be misinterpreted or
misunderstood. In such cases, a special kind of
gentleness is required, one that allows time for
trust to develop.

Giving

"If there is among you a poor man, one of your brethren, in any of your towns within your land which the LORD your God gives you, you shall not harden your heart or shut your hand against your poor brother, but you shall open your hand to him, and lend him sufficient for his need, whatever it may be."

Deuteronomy 15:7-8 RSV

Then the ones who pleased the Lord will ask, "When did we give you something to eat or drink? When did we welcome you as a stranger or give you clothes to wear or visit you while you were sick or in jail?" The king will answer, "Whenever you did it for any of my people, no matter how unimportant they seemed, you did it for me."

Matthew 25:37-40 CEV

In everything I did, I showed you that by this kind of hard work we must help the weak, remembering the words the Lord Jesus himself said: "It is more blessed to give than to receive."

Acts 20:35

God has given gifts to each of you from his great variety of spiritual gifts. Manage them well so that God's generosity can flow through you.

1 Peter 4:10 NLT

Examples Make Great Gifts

At a church meeting a very wealthy man rose to tell the rest of those present about his Christian faith.

"I'm a millionaire," he said, "and I attribute it all to the rich blessings of God in my life. I remember the turning point in my faith. I had just earned my first dollar and I went to a church meeting that night. The speaker was a missionary who told about his work. I knew that I had only a dollar bill, and either had to give it all to God's work or give nothing at all. So at that moment I decided to give all I had to God. I believe God blessed that decision, and that is why I am a rich man today."

As he finished, an awed quiet settled upon the congregation. Then just as he had seated himself, the voice of a little boy broke the silence: "I dare you to do it again."

At an early age, children need to experience sharing with others the blessings they receive from God. Look for a way today to set an example that demonstrates to your child your belief that it is more blessed to give than to receive.

Giving

"But who am I and who are my people that we should be able to offer as generously as this? For all things come from Thee, and from Thy hand we have given Thee."

1 Chronicles 29:14 NASB

Jesus went over to the collection box in the Temple and sat and watched as the crowds dropped in their money. Many rich people put in large amounts. Then a poor widow came and dropped in two pennies. He called his disciples to him and said, "I assure you, this poor widow has given more than all the others have given. For they gave a tiny part of their surplus, but she, poor as she is, has given everything she has."

Mark 12:41-44 NLT

God did not keep back his own Son, but he gave him for us. If God did this, won't he freely give us everything else?

Romans 8:32 CEV

If I give all I possess to the poor and surrender my body to the flames, but have not love, I gain nothing.

1 Corinthians 13:3

A Generous Spirit Can Change Your World

Chad was a shy, quiet little boy. One day he came home and told his parents he wanted to make a valentine for everyone in his class. That night his dad and mom talked about it. Chad wasn't very popular. The other kids didn't include him in their games. He always walked home by himself. What if he went to all the trouble and then didn't receive any Valentines?

They decided to encourage him anyway. For three weeks, for hours after school, Chad worked until he had made thirty-five valentines.

Valentine's Day dawned, and Chad excitedly put his handiwork into a paper bag and bolted out the door. Trying to be prepared for his disappointment, Chad's parents had plans to take him out for ice cream that night.

That afternoon, Chad came running home, all out of breath. His arms were empty. His folks expected him to burst into tears. "Not a one, not a one," Chad said, over and over. His mom and dad looked at him and held each other.

Then he added, "I didn't forget a single kid."

One of the beautiful benefits of being generous toward others is that it's so rewarding it changes the way we look at the world.

Grace

I pray that the LORD will bless and protect you, and that he will show you mercy and kindness.

Numbers 6:24-25 CEV

"And I have also given you what you have not asked, both riches and honor, so that there will not be any among the kings like you all your days. And if you walk in My ways, keeping My statutes and commandments, as you father David walked, then I will prolong your days."

1 Kings 3:13-14 NASB

Praise the LORD, I tell myself; with my whole heart, I will praise his holy name. Praise the LORD, I tell myself, and never forget the good things he does for me.

Psalm 103:1-2 NLT

But by the grace of God I am what I am, and his grace to me was not without effect. No, I worked harder than all of them—yet not I, but the grace of God that was with me.

1 Corinthians 15:10

Making a List of Favors

After Robinson Crusoe was shipwrecked and stranded on a desert island, he began to take stock of his condition. He drew up two columns, in one he noted what he called the evils and in the other he wrote the goods that he faced.

He was cast onto a desolate island—but he was still alive, unlike the rest of his ship's company.

He had no human companions—but he was not starving.

He was wearing only rags—but with the warm climate he did not need more.

He had no means of defending himself— but he saw no wild beasts.

He had no way of preparing food—but the disabled ship had drifted close enough to shore that he could retrieve necessary provisions.

By the time he finished his notes, Crusoe concluded that there are no situations in life so miserable but that one could find something for which to be grateful.

"Gratitude is an attitude," as the saying goes. Suppose you were to recall a situation in your life when you faced a serious crisis—of health, work, or relationship. And suppose you could make a list similar to that of Robinson Crusoe's. Would your awareness of God's grace in your life be as clear?

Grace

LORD, you have assigned me my portion and my cup; you have made my lot secure. The boundary lines have fallen for me in pleasant places; surely I have a delightful inheritance.

Psalm 16:5-6

Better is a little with the fear of the LORD than great treasure and trouble with it.

Proverbs 15:16 RSV

For where your treasure is, there will your heart be also.

Luke 12:34 KJV

Oh, what a wonderful God we have! How great are his riches and wisdom and knowledge! How impossible it is for us to understand his decisions and his methods!

Romans 11:33 NLT

Your Most Prized Possession

A family was traveling down the highway when
the car ahead of them lost a suitcase that had been
tied on top. They stopped to pick it up, then tried
unsuccessfully to catch up with the other car.

Looking inside the suitcase, they found a clue
to the owner's identity—a twenty-dollar gold
piece inscribed with the words, "Awarded to Otis
Sampson by the Portland Cement Company."

After communicating with the company, the
father contacted Mr. Sampson. A delighted
Sampson said they could discard the contents, but
he'd like the gold piece, which he called "my most
prized possession."

The father sent the gold piece, and included a
letter in which he told about his own "most
prized possession," his faith in Jesus Christ.

Sometime later, a package arrived from the
Sampsons. In it was the twenty-dollar gold piece,
along with a note, which said, "We want you to
have this gold piece. We have become believers in
Christ. I am seventy-four; my wife is seventy-two.
You were the first to tell us about the Savior. Now
He is our most prized possession."

What is the most prized possession that you'd
like to pass along to your children? Is it earthy
gold, or heavenly grace?

Gratitude

Let us come into his presence with thanksgiving; let us make a joyful noise to him with songs of praise!

Psalm 95:2 RSV

Each one of you is part of the body of Christ, and you were chosen to live together in peace. So let the peace that comes from Christ control your thoughts. And be grateful.

Colossians 3:15 CEV

Thank God for his gift that is too wonderful for words!

2 Corinthians 9:15 CEV

Sing and make music in your heart to the Lord, always giving thanks to God the Father for everything, in the name of our Lord Jesus Christ.

Ephesians 5:19-20

Thanks for Your Call—Even If It's Collect

A father once found this note pinned to the bulletin board by the family phone:

> Daddy—I am going to wash my hair. If Tom calls, tell him to call at eight. If Herb calls and Tom doesn't, tell Herb to call at eight, but if they both call, tell Herb to call at 8:15 or 8:30. If Timmy calls, and Tom and Herb don't, tell Timmy to call at eight, but if they both call (Tom & Herb) or one calls, tell Timmy to call at 8:30 or 8:40.
>
> —Tina

If you're scratching your head about how to be grateful about something like this, consider:

The Illinois Bell Telephone Company reports that the volume of long-distance calls being made on Father's Day is growing. They also report that most of the calls to fathers on Father's Day were made "collect."

Still wondering where the gratitude comes in? Well, be grateful first that your daughter is preparing to leave home some day, and one of those Toms or Herbs or Timmys may be your future son-in-law. And secondly, you can be grateful if your daughter is among those away from home and busily starting out on her own, who still remembers your special day.

Gratitude

It is good to give thanks to the Lord, to sing praises to the Most High. It is good to proclaim your unfailing love in the morning, your faithfulness in the evening.

Psalm 92:1-2 NLT

But thanks be to God! He gives us the victory through our Lord Jesus Christ.

1 Corinthians 15:57

Now I rejoice in my sufferings for your sake, and in my flesh I complete what is lacking in Christ's afflictions for the sake of his body, that is, the church.

Colossians 1:24 RSV

We pray this so that the name of our Lord Jesus may be glorified in you, and you in Him, according to the grace of our God and the Lord Jesus Christ.

2 Thessalonians 1:12-13

Giving Thanks for Pests

Surely the most unusual monument in America is to be found in the town of Enterprise, Coffee County, Alabama. There on the town square is a statue expressing the gratitude of the local people for the Mexican boll weevil.

In 1895, the boll weevil arrived in large numbers and wiped out the year's cotton crop, the major economic basis for much of the South at the time. In desperation, the farmers searched for other crops to plant, and by 1919 the county's peanut crop yield was many times what cotton had brought at its height. In gratitude for that year of prosperity, a fountain and monument were built.

The inscription reads:

> *In profound appreciation of the boll weevil*
> *And what it has done as the herald of prosperity,*
> *This monument was erected by the citizens*
> *Of Enterprise, Coffee County, Alabama.*

The ability to find blessing in adversity is one of our most valuable gifts. Perhaps an opportunity will arise today to help your child out of a frustrating situation by turning it into an opportunity for imagination, adventure, and thanksgiving.

Grief

The Lord therefore said to Moses, "Gather for Me seventy men from the elders of Israel, whom you know to be the elders of the people and their officers and bring them to the tent of meeting, and let them take their stand there with you. Then I will come down and speak with you there, and I will take of the Spirit who is upon you, and will put Him upon them; and they shall bear the burden of the people with you, so that you shall not bear it all alone."

Numbers 11:16-17 NASB

For his anger lasts only a moment, but his favor lasts a lifetime; weeping may remain for a night, but rejoicing comes in the morning.

Psalm 30:5

The Lord has sent me to comfort those who mourn, especially in Jerusalem. He sent me to give them flowers in place of their sorrow, olive oil in place of tears, and joyous praise in place of broken hearts.

Isaiah 61:2-3 CEV

Then Jesus wept.

John 11:35 NLT

A Grief Shared

Some years ago columnist Alexander Woolcott described this scene in a New York hospital:

A mother sat in the hospital lounge in silence, tears streaming down her cheeks. The head nurse comforted her about the death, just moments before, of her only child.

The nurse asked her, "Did you see the little boy sitting in the hall as you left your daughter's room?" No, the mother said, she had not noticed him.

His mother had been brought to the hospital by ambulance a few days earlier. Recent immigrants, they knew no one in the city. Every day and night the little boy sat outside his mother's room.

"Fifteen minutes ago that little boy's mother died," the nurse continued, "and now I must go tell this child that he is all alone in the world."

Then the nurse added, "I don't suppose you would go with me?"

The grieving mother looked up in shock, but dried her tears, straightened her hair, and went with the nurse. Not only that, she put her arms around the boy and invited him to come home with her.

They soon came to know the meaning of the promise: a grief shared is a burden lightened.

Grief

Yea, though I walk through the valley of the shadow of death, I will fear no evil: for thou art with me; thy rod and thy staff they comfort me.

Psalm 23:4 KJV

Set me as a seal upon your heart, as a seal upon your arm; for love is strong as death, jealousy is cruel as the grave. Its flashes are flashes of fire, a most vehement flame.

Song of Solomon 8:6 RSV

"I tell you the truth, if anyone keeps my word, he will never see death."

John 8:51

I heard a loud voice shout from the throne: God's home is now with his people. He will live with them, and they will be his own. Yes, God will make his home among his people. He will wipe all tears from their eyes, and there will be no more death, suffering, crying, or pain. These things of the past are gone forever.

Revelation 21:3-4 CEV

Healing Grief's Wounds

Over recent months, a young boy had gradually begun to understand that he'd never get to play like other boys. And lately, he'd begun to bring up the subject of death.

One day, the little boy asked,

"Mama, what is it like to die? Mama, does it hurt?"

Quick tears flooded her eyes. She took a deep breath, and uttered a brief prayer for wisdom.

"Kenneth," she said, "do you remember when you used to play so hard that when night came you were too tired to undress, and you'd tumble into your mother's bed and fall asleep? Next morning, you'd wake up and find yourself in your own bed, because someone loved you and took care of you?

"Darling, death is something like that," she said softly. "Some day we all wake up to find ourselves in another room—a room where we belong, with the Lord who loves us."

The boy smiled and soon fell asleep in her arms. Not many weeks later he fell asleep just as she said, trusting that his Father in heaven would take him to his new room.

Grief is the inevitable wound that accompanies loss. Healing for that wound comes from trusting that the one we love is in the Lord's embrace.

Guidance

He makes me lie down in green pastures, he leads me beside quiet waters, he restores my soul. He guides me in paths of righteousness for his name's sake.

Psalm 23:2-3

Don't let anyone make fun of you, just because you are young. Set an example for other followers by what you say and do, as well as by your love, faith, and purity.

1 Timothy 4:12 CEV

Don't lord it over the people assigned to your care, but lead by your good example.

1 Peter 5:3 NLT

What you have learned and received and heard and seen in me, do; and the God of peace will be with you.

Philippians 4:9 RSV

Showing a More Excellent Way

Grandpa came into the room where his grandson Joey was in his playpen, crying his heart out and jumping up and down. When Joey saw his grandfather, he reached out his chubby arms and cried all the louder, "Out, Gampa, out!"

Grandpa naturally reached down to Joey, but as he did, Joey's mother arrived to say, "No, Dad, Joey is being punished. He has to stay in his playpen."

Grandpa felt at a loss to know what to do. He didn't want to overrule his daughter's efforts to discipline her son. Yet Joey's tears and uplifted hands tugged at his heart.

Suddenly Grandpa had an idea. If he couldn't take Joey out of the playpen, there was no rule against climbing in there himself. And that's just what he did—to Joey's instant delight, and to Joey's mother's grudging smile.

Grandpa found a way to administer justice with mercy. Guidance in its finest form means "directing toward a better way." It goes beyond the kind of punishment that brings pain without lessons learned. Guidance means instilling in a child a desire to make a better choice of behaviors. On this occasion, both Grandpa's daughter and grandson benefited from his wise example.

Guidance

O God, Thou hast taught me from my youth;
And I still declare Thy wondrous deeds.
Psalm 71:17 NASB

Say to wisdom, "Your are my sister," and call
understanding your kinsman.
Proverbs 7:4

How much better to get wisdom than gold, and
understanding than silver!
Proverbs 16:16 NLT

Then he answered and spake unto me, saying,
This is the word of The LORD unto Zerubbabel,
saying, Not by might, nor by power, but by my
spirit, saith the LORD of hosts.
Zechariah 4:6 KJV

What Did You Learn Today?

The late TV lecturer and best-selling author Leo Buscaglia often said this about the guidance he received from his father:

"Papa believed that the greatest sin was to go to bed at night as ignorant as when we awakened."

"Papa insisted that each child learn one new thing each day. Dinnertime was the forum for sharing new facts and insights. At the end of the meal came the question asked solemnly of each child, 'Tell me what you learned today.' Before the meal was over, the entire family had been enlightened by at least half a dozen facts.

"The news we recounted, no matter how insignificant, was never taken lightly. Mama and Papa listened carefully and were ready with some comment, often profound and analytical, always to the point.

"In retrospect, I realize what a dynamic educational technique Papa was offering us. Without being aware of it, our family was growing together, sharing experiences, and participating in one another's education. And by listening to us, respecting our input, affirming our value, and giving us a sense of dignity, Papa unquestionably was our most influential teacher."

Think of the guidance we can offer, just by asking the simple question, "What did you learn today?"

Guilt

Where is another God like you, who pardons the sins of the survivors among his people? You cannot stay angry with your people forever, because you delight in showing mercy.

Micah 7:18 NLT

Forgive us for doing wrong, as we forgive others.

Matthew 6:12 CEV

Brethren, if a man is overtaken in any trespass, you who are spiritual should restore him in a spirit of gentleness. Look to yourself, lest you too be tempted.

Galatians 6:1 RSV

Get rid of all bitterness, rage and anger, brawling and slander, along with every form of malice. Be kind and compassionate to one another, forgiving each other, just as in Christ God forgave you.

Ephesians 4:31-32

Showing Children How To Forgive . . . Themselves

A couple was at their wits' end. They did not know what to do about their sons' behavior. The mother had heard that a local clergyman was successful in working with difficult children, so she asked her husband if he thought they should talk with the minister.

The husband said, "We might as well. We've got to do something!"

The clergyman agreed to speak with the boys, but asked to see them individually. The eight-year-old went to meet with him first. The clergyman asked him sternly, "Where is God?"

The boy made no response, so the clergyman repeated the question in an even sterner tone, "Where is God?"

Again the boy made no attempt to answer. So the clergyman raised his voice even more and shook his finger in the boy's face, "WHERE IS GOD?"

At that the boy bolted from the room and ran straight home, slamming himself in the closet.

His older brother called to him and said, "What happened?"

The younger brother replied, "We're in BIG trouble this time. God is missing, and they think we did it."

Children sometimes possess a greater sense of guilt than we realize. As fathers, we can reassure them that God is a source of comfort, not fear.

Guilt

You are kind, God! Please have pity on me. You
are always merciful! Please wipe away my sins.
Wash me clean from all of my sin and guilt.

Psalm 51:1-2 CEV

Let the redeemed of the LORD say so, Whom He
has redeemed from the hand of the adversary.

Psalm 107:2 NASB

And Zacchaeus stood, and said unto the Lord;
Behold, Lord, the half of my goods I give to the
poor; and if I have taken any thing from any man
by false accusation, I restore him fourfold.

Luke 19:8 KJV

When we were utterly helpless, Christ came at just
the right time and died for us sinners. Now, no
one is likely to die for a good person, though
someone might be willing to die for a person who
is especially good. But God showed his great love
for us by sending Christ to die for us while we
were still sinners.

Romans 5:6-8 NLT

Redeem Your Regrets

His name still conjures up memories of booming home runs, blazing speed, inspiring natural ability—and images of life on the wild side.

Near the end of his life, Mickey Mantle received a liver transplant after years of alcohol abuse. Even in this difficult situation, graciousness toned his words, as Mantle told the media:

"You talk about your role models. This is your role model—don't be like me."

Mantle squarely faced the fact that while he had been a superstar on the field, he could not commend his personal life to the young for emulation.

Nevertheless, in the ninth inning of his life, Mantle hit a personal home run. He pleaded eloquently with others to take heed of his mistakes. In return, during his final days, fans new and old showered him with an outpouring of love—in response to both his great baseball heroics, and his honest self-appraisal of personal pain and regret.

Because of his pleas, organ donations increased virtually overnight all across America, giving countless people what Mantle himself did not enjoy—extra innings.

Regrets about our mistakes need not paralyze us in guilt. Even our faults can bless others when we courageously acknowledge them and graciously accept the blessings of a second chance.

Happiness

To everyone who is thirsty, he gives something to drink; to everyone who is hungry, he gives good things to eat.

Psalm 107:9 CEV

Better is a little with righteousness than great revenues without right.

Proverbs 16:8 KJV

Better is an handful with quietness, than both the hands full with travail and vexation of spirit.

Ecclesiastes 4:6 KJV

Not that I complain of want; for I have learned, in whatever state I am, to be content.

Philippians 4:11 RSV

Eight Requirements for Contented Living

Health enough
to make work a pleasure.

Wealth enough
to support your needs.

Strength enough
to battle with difficulties and overcome them.

Grace enough
to confess your sins and put them behind you.

Patience enough
to toil until some good is accomplished.

Faith enough
to make real the things of God.

Hope enough
to remove all anxious fear about the future.

Charity enough
to see some good in everyone.

Johann Wolfgang von Goethe

Happiness

How blessed is the one whom Thou dost choose,
and bring near to Thee, to dwell in Thy courts.

Psalm 65:4 NASB

It is possible to give freely and become more
wealthy, but those who are stingy will lose
everything.

Proverbs 11:24 NLT

A generous man will himself be blessed, for he
shares his food with the poor.

Proverbs 22:9

Warn the rich people of this world not to be
proud or to trust in wealth that is easily lost. Tell
them to have faith in God, who is rich and blesses
us with everything we need to enjoy life. Instruct
them to do as many good deeds as they can and
to help everyone. Remind the rich to be generous
and share what they have. This will lay a solid
foundation for the future, so that they will know
what true life is like.

1 Timothy 6:17-19 CEV

The Secret of Happiness

One day, feeling especially sad and lonely, a little girl named Sabrina took a walk through a meadow, where she noticed a small butterfly caught by its wings on a sharp thorn bush. Carefully, Sabrina released it. Suddenly, the butterfly changed into a lovely good fairy.

"For your wonderful kindness," the good fairy said to Sabrina, "I will tell you the secret of happiness." The fairy whispered something in her ear and then vanished.

As Sabrina grew up, everyone loved to be around her, and often coaxed her to tell them the secret of her happiness. She would tell about the fairy but never about the secret.

Finally, when she was very old and on her deathbed, Sabrina gathered the neighbors around her and told them, "I do not want the secret of happiness to die with me, and so I will tell it to you. "Tell us, tell us," they pleaded.

"She told me that everyone, no matter how old or young, rich or poor, no matter how secure they seemed, would have need of me."

The need to be needed is one of humanity's greatest needs. If you can find ways for people to be needed by others, you will find lasting happiness for yourself.

Hope

Hope deferred makes the heart sick, but when dreams come true, there is life and joy.

Proverbs 13:12 NLT

Not only so, but we also rejoice in our sufferings, because we know that suffering produces perseverance; perseverance, character; and character, hope. And hope does not disappoint us, because God has poured out his love into our hearts by the Holy Spirit, whom he has given us.

Romans 5:3-5

Now may the God of hope fill you with all joy and peace in believing, that you may abound in hope by the power of the Holy Spirit.

Romans 15:13 NASB

Praise God, the Father of our Lord Jesus Christ. God is so good, and by raising Jesus from death, he has given us new life and a hope that lives on.

1 Peter 1:3 CEV

Keep Your Hope Alive

Bob Ritchie is a former truck driver and ex-Marine—not the kind of guy you'd expect to see in a hospital ward with a child in his lap.

But Ritchie retired early and soon found that having nothing to do got on his nerves. So he decided to create his own volunteer job at St. Christopher's Hospital for Children in Philadelphia. There he makes beds, picks up toys, changes diapers—whatever needs to be done.

Bob started his volunteer work after his own hospitalization. A three-packs-a-day smoker for thirty years, he lost a lung to cancer. During his recovery, he says, "My wife stayed with me the whole time. That's when I realized how important it is to have somebody there."

Bob gets the most satisfaction sitting for hours rocking infants crying in pain. Next comes walking toddlers up and down the hall to work off their energy. While being around children with devastating diseases might not seem like the best place for a man battling cancer, Ritchie sees it differently.

"Being here keeps my mind off my problems. These kids—they're the real heroes."

Seeing children fighting for their lives gives Bob Ritchie what he needs to keep his own hope alive.

Hope

It is of the LORD'S mercies that we are not
consumed, because his compassions fail not. They
are new every morning: great is thy faithfulness.
The LORD is my portion, saith my soul; therefore
will I hope in him.

Lamentations 3:22-24 KJV

I consider that our present sufferings are not
worth comparing with the glory that will be
revealed in us. The creation waits in eager
expectation for the sons of God to be revealed.

Romans 8:18-19

Now we see things imperfectly as in a poor mirror,
but then we will see everything with perfect
clarity. All that I know now is partial and
incomplete, but then I will know everything
completely, just as God knows me now.

1 Corinthians 13:12 NLT

Brethren, I do not consider that I have made it
my own; but one thing I do, forgetting what lies
behind and straining forward to what lies ahead, I
press on toward the goal for the prize of the
upward call of God in Christ Jesus.

Philippians 3:13-14 RSV

Hope Means: The Best Is Yet to Be

At Columbia University, John Erskine was considered one of their greatest teachers ever. He was a true "Renaissance man"—author of sixty books, accomplished concert pianist, head of the Julliard School of Music, and a popular and witty lecturer.

Students flocked to Erskine's courses, not because of his fame or his accomplishments, but because his excitement for learning was contagious. He was possessed of a conviction that the world did not belong to him, but to his students.

Over and over he would remind them, "The best books are yet to be written. The best paintings have not yet been painted. The best governments are yet to be formed."

"The best is yet to be done—by you!"

Indeed, hundreds of John Erskine's students have gone into the world as leaders in every aspect of music as teachers, performers, and composers. Others have become writers, painters, and political leaders. Many attribute their achievements and dreams to this mentor's reminder that the best is yet to be.

Hope, according to Erich Fromm, means "to be ready at every moment for that which is not yet born." By reminding our children of this, and by living in hope ourselves, we do our part to assure their future greatness.

Integrity

Speaking the truth in love, we are to grow up in all aspects into Him, who is the head, even Christ, from whom the whole body, being fitted and held together by that which every joint supplies, according to the proper working of each individual part, causes the growth of the body for the building up of itself in love.

Ephesians 4:15-16 NASB

Therefore put on the full armor of God, so that when the day of evil comes, you may be able to stand your ground, and after you have done everything, to stand.

Ephesians 6:13

May the God of peace himself sanctify you wholly; and may your spirit and soul and body be kept sound and blameless at the coming of our Lord Jesus Christ.

1 Thessalonians 5:23 RSV

When I was first put on trial, no one helped me. In fact, everyone deserted me. I hope it won't be held against them. But the Lord stood beside me. He gave me the strength to tell his full message, so that all Gentiles would hear it. And I was kept safe from hungry lions.

2 Timothy 4:16-17 CEV

Integrity Means Wholeness

As coach of the St. Anthony Friars High School basketball team, Bob Hurley has a stunning record—517 wins against only 60 losses, with 15 state championships, five Top Ten rankings, and one national championship as of 1993.

Of greater importance to Hurley are these records: nearly half of his varsity players routinely make the honor roll, and all but one of his players have gone on to college, where approximately 60 percent have graduated.

Hurley helps his players choose a college based on academics first, athletics second. He declares his players ineligible if their grades suffer: "If you're not committed to your own education, how can your teammates trust your commitment to them?"

On the court, Hurley is impatient, noisy, and a strict disciplinarian. Off the court, he often invites players who are struggling with their grades to come to dinner at his home—and stay for tutoring sessions.

Coach Hurley has received coaching offers from numerous coaches. But Jersey City is home for him. In 1992, the city honored him with a banquet and accolades from celebrities. The next day he was out helping players find summer jobs.

The dictionary definition of *integrity* involves wholeness of mind, body, and spirit. Coach Hurley is a walking example of it.

Integrity

My lips will not speak wickedness, and my tongue
will utter no deceit. I will never admit you are in
the right; till I die, I will not deny my integrity.
Job 27:4-5

But as for me, I will walk in mine integrity:
redeem me, and be merciful unto me.
Psalm 26:11 KJV

It is better to be poor and honest than to be a
fool and dishonest.
Proverbs 19:1 NLT

Dear friends, God is good. So I beg you to offer
your bodies to him as a living sacrifice, pure and
pleasing. That's the most sensible way to serve
God. Don't be like the people of this world, but
let God change the way you think. Then you will
know how to do everything that is good and
pleasing to him.
Romans 12:1-2 CEV

Patrons and Profits

Adrian Thomas held a bonfire out behind the drug store in Meyersdale, Pennsylvania, which his family had operated for three generations.

One winter day in 1992, he came to a fateful decision. He had seen too many deaths of friends caused by cancer and heart disease. For ninety-six years, his family had sold tobacco products, prominently displayed at the front of the store, ironically, positioned ahead of the health products.

That day, Thomas, his family members, and employees boxed up $2,000 worth of cigarettes, cigars, snuff, and pipe-tobacco products and piled them in the middle of the parking lot. Thomas first struck a match to his state tobacco license, which he used to torch the pile.

As the growing crowd watched the stash go up in smoke, Thomas told local media he could no longer put profits above the health of his patrons.

Some might scoff that the actions of Adrian Thomas made no difference in the smoking habits of the country, and that some other store quickly would absorb the sales. But Thomas didn't base his decision on economics. He was responding to a sense of his own integrity. He leaves it to other tobacco sellers to decide what they should do.

Jealousy

But when his brothers saw that their father loved him more than all his brothers, they hated him, and could not speak peaceably to him. Now Joseph had a dream, and when he told it to his brothers they only hated him the more.

Genesis 37:4-5 RSV

Don't hold grudges. On the other hand, it's wrong not to correct someone who needs correcting. Stop being angry and don't try to take revenge. I am the LORD, and I command you to love others as much as you love yourself.

Leviticus 19:17-18 CEV

Do not fret because of evil men or be envious of those who do wrong.

Psalm 37:1

And they began to argue among themselves as to who would be the greatest in the coming Kingdom. Jesus told them, "In this world the kings and great men order their people around, and yet they are called 'friends of the people.' But among you, those who are the greatest should take the lowest rank, and the leader should be like a servant.

Luke 22:24-26 NLT

Blind Jealousy and Blind Justice

A wealthy man died, apparently without leaving a will. According to law, his estate was divided among surviving relatives through a public auction.

During the auction, three distant cousins who had fought for years began to bid, often competing with each other. This only drove up the price.

Toward the end, the auctioneer held up a dusty framed photograph, but no one bid on it. Finally a woman approached the auctioneer and asked if she could buy it for a dollar, which is all she had. She said she had been a servant of the wealthy man, and recognized the picture—it was of the deceased man's only son, who had died trying to rescue a drowning child.

The auctioneer accepted the dollar, and the woman went home and started to place the photograph on a table beside her bed. Then she noticed a bulge in the back of the frame. She undid the backing, and there, to her amazement, was the rich man's will.

His instructions were simple: "I bequeath all my possessions to whomever cares enough for my son to cherish this photograph."

Jealousy can blind us to what truly matters, as surely as any disease of our eyes.

Jealousy

"You shall not make for yourself a graven image, or any likeness of anything that is in heaven above, or that is in the earth beneath, or that is in the water under the earth; you shall not bow down to them or serve them; for I the LORD your God am a jealous God."

Exodus 20:4-5 RSV

So the angel who was speaking with me said to me, "Proclaim, saying, 'Thus says the LORD of hosts, "I am exceedingly jealous for Jerusalem and Zion."'"

Zechariah 1:14 NASB

A jealous husband can be furious and merciless when he takes revenge. He won't let you pay him off, no matter what you offer.

Proverbs 6:34-35 CEV

Seeing ye have purified your souls in obeying the truth through the Spirit unto unfeigned love of the brethren, see that ye love one another with a pure heart fervently.

1 Peter 1:22 KJV

A Jump Start to Jealousy

Marie was suffering from depression, or so her husband Jerry thought. He took her to a psychiatrist to confirm that the problem was hers and not his.

The doctor listened to the couple talk about their relationship, and he soon realized that what their marriage needed was simply a rekindling of their early love.

However, the relationship needed some shock therapy, a jump-start, to reawaken Jerry's feelings for Marie.

The doctor announced, "The treatment I prescribe is really quite simple."

With that he went over to Marie, gathered her up in his arms, and gave her a big kiss. As he stepped back, he looked at her glowing face and big smile. Then he glanced at Jerry, expecting to see an expression of jealousy, and saw instead the same blank look he came in with.

"I'm sorry I had to do this," the doctor said to Jerry, "but I wanted to show you this is all Marie needs to give her back the life you once enjoyed together."

"That's fine, Doc," said Jerry. "I can bring her in on Tuesdays and Thursdays."

Sometimes a healthy dose of jealousy is a sign that people truly care about each other. A relationship without it may be in the worst shape of all.

Justice

"You shall not pervert the justice due to the sojourner or to the fatherless, or take a widow's garment in pledge; but you shall remember that you were a slave in Egypt and the LORD your God redeemed you from there; therefore I command you to do this."

Deuteronomy 24:17-18 RSV

The LORD is more pleased when we do what is just and right than when we give him sacrifices.

Proverbs 21:3 NLT

Woe to those who enact evil statutes, And to those who constantly record unjust decisions, So as to deprive the needy of justice, and rob the poor of My people of their rights, In order that widows may be their spoil, And that they may plunder the orphans.

Isaiah 10:1-2 NASB

He has showed you, O man, what is good. And what does the LORD require of you? To act justly and to love mercy and to walk humbly with your God.

Micah 6:8

Good Old-Fashioned Justice

Novelist John Grisham, author of several best-selling books that became blockbuster movies, has been called "a straight arrow making his way along a very crooked path."

Grisham's novels often depict as villains sleazy lawyers, corrupt politicians, and trigger-happy officers—the underbelly of a world of wealth and respectability. His heroes, on the other hand, are generally the guileless and innocent, including children. An eleven-year-old boy was the main character in *The Client*.

He refuses to write anything, he says, that would offend or embarrass either his mother or his children. Contrary to what many in the entertainment world might have predicted, Grisham's approach has paid off—big. *The Firm* now has 19 million copies in print. All his other works come off the presses with million-plus first editions. So far, the oldest fan to write him was ninety-six years old, and the youngest was ten. Many readers commend him for creating such exciting stories without graphic violence, obscenities, and profanities. One woman wrote that his were the only novels her husband had read in seventeen years.

Could it be that all the sex and gore is just a cheap distraction? Apparently people hunger for a good old-fashioned tale of good versus evil, with justice winning in the end.

Justice

The wicked don't care about the rights of the poor, but good people do.

Proverbs 29:7 CEV

And whosoever shall give to drink unto one of these little ones a cup of cold water only in the name of a disciple, verily I say unto you, he shall in no wise lose his reward.

Matthew 10:42 KJV

"The Spirit of the Lord is upon me, because he has anointed me to preach good news to the poor. He has sent me to proclaim release to the captives and recovering of sight to the blind, to set a liberty those who are oppressed."

Luke 4:18 RSV

You know how full of love and kindness of Lord Jesus Christ was. Though he was very rich, yet for your sakes he became poor, so that by his poverty he could make you rich.

2 Corinthians 8:9 NLT

Doing Justice Is a Privilege

When Dr. Pedro Jose Greer looks at his medical career, he says, "I've had the privilege of treating the sick," he says, "and the honor of working with the poor."

Privilege? Honor? Not the usual contexts for those words.

Dr. Greer traces a change in his view of life to 1984, when as an intern he treated a homeless man for tuberculosis. A usually curable disease, it had progressed to a fatal stage. Greer was appalled that someone could be so poor and ignorant as to neglect medical treatment. Greer spent four days searching the streets for the man's family, hoping the man wouldn't die alone.

Rather than bemoan this one case, Greer took action. He set up a clinic in a shelter—beginning with only a folding table. He took other doctors along with him. Today his Camillus Health Concern is one of the largest providers of medical care for the poor in South Florida, treating 4,500 patients a year.

Greer has won numerous awards for his humanitarian effort. But he has never forgotten that homeless man who died alone. Though he could earn more in a more lucrative practice, it's worth it, he says, for the "privilege" and the "honor" of blending his healing with justice.

Loneliness

In peace I will both lie down and sleep, For Thou alone, O LORD, dost make me to dwell in safety.

Psalm 4:8 NASB

Thou dost show me the path of life; in thy presence there is fulness of joy, in thy right hand are pleasures for evermore.

Psalm 16:11 RSV

You find families for those who are lonely. You set prisoners free and let them prosper, but all who rebel will live in a scorching desert.

Psalm 68:6 CEV

Where can I go from your Spirit? Where can I flee from your presence? . . . If I say, "Surely the darkness will hide me and the light become night around me," even the darkness will not be dark to you; the night will shine like the day, for darkness is as light to you.

Psalm 139:7,11-12

My Daddy Is Here

David Elkind, the famous child psychologist and author of the best-selling *The Hurried Child*, tells this true story about his role as a parent:

I remember visiting my middle son's nursery school class, at the request of his teacher, so that I could observe a 'problem child' in the class. It so happened that I was sitting and observing a group of boys, including my son, who sat in a circle nearby.

Their conversation went like this:

Child A: "My daddy is a doctor, and he makes a lot of money and we have a swimming pool."

Child B: "My daddy is a lawyer, and he flies to Washington and talks to the president."

Child C: "My daddy owns a company, and we have our own airplane."

Then my son (with aplomb, of course): "My daddy is here!"

Elkind went on to stress the harmful effects to your children of your absence at school functions. Children regard the public presence of their parents as a visible symbol of caring and connectedness. He writes, "That is far more significant than any material support could ever be." Do you know the date of your child's next big school event? Will you be there?

Loneliness

I lie down and sleep; I wake again, because the LORD sustains me.

Psalm 3:5

I can lie down and sleep soundly because you, LORD, will keep me safe.

Psalm 4:8 CEV

My people will live in safety, quietly at home. They will be at rest.

Isaiah 32:18 NLT

As one whom his mother comforts, so I will comfort you; you shall be comforted in Jerusalem.

Isaiah 66:13 RSV

A Lap for Loneliness

One of Howard Maxwell's Christmas gifts to his four-year-old daughter Melinda was a colorful edition of "The Three Little Pigs."

Soon Melinda acquired a fixation for her new gift, and insisted that her daddy read it to her every night at bedtime.

Maxwell eventually tired of the story and had an idea. He purchased a child's easy-to-use tape recorder and read the story onto a tape for her. The next night, when Melinda asked her father to read, he showed her how to press the "Play" button.

At first she was fascinated at the novelty of her father's voice coming from a machine, and she even learned how to use the playback button. This worked for a couple of nights, and then Melinda firmly handed the storybook to her father.

"But honey," he said, "you know how to turn on the recorder."

"Yes," said Melinda, "but I can't sit on its lap."

In spite of the temporary excitement that a child receives from learning to play with the latest electronically correct toy, in the long run such objects create a sense of isolation, if not loneliness. Sometimes the only appropriate way to play is with a huggable parent.

Loss

He healeth the broken in heart, and bindeth up
their wounds.

Psalm 147:3 KJV

"I will seek the lost, bring back the scattered, bind
up the broken, and strengthen the sick; but the fat
and the strong I will destroy. I will feed them with
judgment."

Ezekiel 34:16 NASB

Then he asked me, "Son of man, can these bones
become living people again?" "O Sovereign
LORD," I replied, "you alone know the answer to
that." Then he said to me, "Speak to these bones
and say, 'Dry bones, listen to the word of the
LORD! This is what the Sovereign LORD says:
Look! I am going to breathe into you and make
you live again! I will put flesh and muscles on you
and cover you with skin. I will put breath into
you, and you will come to life. Then you will
know that I am the LORD.'"

Ezekiel 37:3-6 NLT

Jesus looked at them and said, "With man this is
impossible, but with God all things are possible."
Matthew 19:26

Strong in the Broken Places

Max Cleland was a typical Southern boy. He starred in sports, was voted his high school's most outstanding senior, and volunteered for combat duty in Vietnam.

One month before heading for home, Lt. Cleland saw a grenade on the ground that somebody had apparently dropped. As he reached to pick it up, the grenade suddenly exploded in his face. Dazed and bleeding, he saw that his right hand and right leg were missing, his left leg badly mangled. He tried to cry out—but shrapnel had ripped his throat.

He was rushed to a medical hospital, but nobody expected him to survive. But as he slowly recovered from a triple amputation, recalling the Apostle Paul's words that "hope does not disappoint" strengthened him.

Upon returning to civilian life, Cleland learned to drive a special car, and entered politics to try to mobilize support for veterans' causes. At age thrity-four, he was named the youngest ever head of the Veterans Administration. Later he became Georgia's secretary of state and now serves as a U.S. Senator.

Along the way, Cleland wrote a book titled *Strong in the Broken Places.* The phrase refers to the way bones often heal and also to the way life responds to loss.

LOSS

We know that in everything God works for good with those who love him, who are called according to his purpose.

Romans 8:28 RSV

And I am convinced that nothing can ever separate us from his love. Death can't, and life can't. The angels can't, and the demons can't. Our fears for today, our worries about tomorrow, and even the powers of hell can't keep God's love away. Whether we are high above the sky or in the deepest ocean, nothing in all creation will ever be able to separate us from the love of God that is revealed in Christ Jesus our Lord.

Romans 8:38-39 NLT

If we live, we live to the Lord; and if we die, we die to the Lord. So, whether we live or die, we belong to the Lord.

Romans 14:8

The bodies we now have are weak and can die. But they will be changed into bodies that are eternal. Then the Scriptures will come true, "Death has lost the battle! Where is its victory? Where is its sting?"

1 Corinthians 15:54-55 CEV

Every Exit Is an Entrance

Author-pastor John Claypool offers a reassuring perspective on the experience of loss:

"I've learned something through all my experiences—that every exit is also an entrance.

"Every time you walk out of something, you walk into something.

"I got into this world by dying in the womb—and it must have been painful to get ripped out of that familiar place—but that was the prerequisite of my getting into time and space.

"At the end of my life in history there's going to be a similar kind of transition experience. If we can get at the terror of death by saying it is a transformer rather than an annihilator, then perhaps we can get rid of the idea that death is a thief and is taking something that is rightfully ours, which is the basis of all the rage that I know."

Death is the ultimate experience of loss, of course, and it often overshadows all our other losses. Watching children grow up and out of our control can cause a painful sense of loss. So can the loss of a job, or being forced to move, or simply growing older.

May we all come to view our losses as "transformers rather than annihilators."

Love

Though I speak with the tongues of men and of angels, and have not charity, I am become as sounding brass, or a tinkling cymbal.

1 Corinthians 13:1 KJV

If I had the gift of prophecy, and if I knew all the mysteries of the future and knew everything about everything, but didn't love others, what good would I be? And if I had the gift of faith so that I could speak to a mountain and make it move, without love I would be no good to anybody.

1 Corinthians 13:2 NLT

What if I gave away all that I owned and let myself be burned alive? I would gain nothing, unless I loved others.

1 Corinthians 13:3 CEV

Love is patient, love is kind. It does not envy, it does no boast, it is not proud. It is not rude, it is not self-seeking, it is not easily angered, it keeps no record of wrongs. Love does not delight in evil but rejoices with the truth. It always protects, always trusts, always hopes, always perseveres.

1 Corinthians 13:4-7

Life-Transforming Love

The poet Robert Browning met the love of his life, Elizabeth Barrett, when both were over forty years old. During her early years, Elizabeth had endured hell on earth. One of eleven children, she grew up under the siege of an oppressive, abusive father. His angry rages frequently confined her to bed with an accumulation of ills.

Then Elizabeth met Robert. He did not see her as a sickly, middle-aged invalid, but as a beautiful, talented spirit waiting to bloom. After some brutal confrontations with her father, they were married and traveled the European continent, drinking in the wonders of centuries-old beauty.

Their union transformed them both. At forty-three, Elizabeth gave birth to her first child. This loving wife and mother at last began to explore her gift for poetry. The collections she wrote, such as *Sonnets from the Portuguese*, celebrate in word portraits the transformation of her life. One of the poems included was the incomparable "How Do I Love Thee?"

The Elizabeth Barrett Browning who became one of our greatest romantic poets was there all the time, just waiting for her lover to discover her. Is someone in your life waiting for your love to bring out her best?

Love

My lover is mine and I am his; he browses among the lilies.

Song of Solomon 2:16 NIV

You have ravished my heart, my treasure, my bride. I am overcome by one glance of your eyes, by a single bead of your necklace. How sweet is your love, my treasure, my bride! How much better it is than wine! Your perfume is more fragrant than the richest of spices.

Song of Solomon 4:9-10 NLT

The fig tree forms its early fruit; the blossoming vines spread their fragrance. Arise, come, my darling; my beautiful one, come with me.

Song of Solomon 2:13

"Put me like a seal over your heart, Like a seal on your arm. For love is as strong as death, Jealousy is as severe as Sheol; Its flashes are flashes of fire, The very flame of the LORD."

Song of Solomon 8:6 NASB

How Do I Love Thee?

How do I love thee? Let me count the ways.
I love thee to the depth and breadth and height
My soul can reach, when feeling out of sight
For the ends of Being and ideal Grace.
I love thee to the level of everyday's
Most quiet need, by sun and candlelight.
I love thee freely, as men strive for Right;
I love thee purely, as they turn from Praise.
I love thee with the passion put to use
In my old griefs, and with my childhood's faith.
I love thee with a love I seemed to lose
With my lost saints!—I love thee with the breath,
Smiles, tears, all of my life!—and if God choose,
I shall but love thee better after death.

Elizabeth Barrett Browning, 1806-1861

As you read the words of this immortal love
poem, consider how you would "count the ways"
you might describe the love of your life. In
silence, picture images of your beloved—at work,
at play, alone, with you, with her children, in
laughter, at prayer. Sometimes words will be given
to you, just when you think words cannot express
your feelings. Feel free to write them and show
them to her.

Marriage

Let thy fountain be blessed: and rejoice with the wife of thy youth. Let her be as the loving hind and pleasant roe; let her breasts satisfy thee at all times; and be thou ravished always with her love.

Proverbs 5:18-19 KJV

There are three things that amaze me—no, four things I do not understand: how an eagle glides through the sky, how a snake slithers on a rock, how a ship navigates the ocean, how a man loves a woman.

Proverbs 30:18-19 NLT

A wife of noble character who can find? She is worth far more than rubies. Her husband has full confidence in her and lacks nothing of value.

Proverbs 31:10-11

She opens her mouth with wisdom, and the teaching of kindness is on her tongue. She looks well to the ways of her household, and does not eat the bread of idleness. Her children rise up and call her blessed; her husband also, and he praises her: "Many women have done excellently, but you surpass them all."

Proverbs 31:26-29 RSV

Killing (and Kindling) with Kindness

Pete sat down with the divorce lawyer. He told such a tale of woe: His wife was a total bore. She always looked a mess, the house was worse, and all she did was complain, especially about him. Now he wanted to make her as miserable as she made him.

"Pete," the lawyer said, "I've got the perfect plan. Go home now, and start treating your wife like a queen. Bring her roses. Take her out for dinner. Tell her how beautiful she looks. And then, just when she's getting used to this treatment, pack your bags. I promise you, nothing will devastate her more."

Pete thought it was a fantastic idea. He couldn't wait to start hatching the plot. He helped her around the house. Breakfast in bed. Weekend getaways. Compliments flowed.

After three weeks, the lawyer called. "I've got the divorce papers ready," he said. "I can make you a free man anytime."

"Are you kidding?" Pete cried. "You wouldn't believe the changes she's made. I'm married to an absolute queen. I wouldn't divorce her in a million years."

This woman who is the mother of your children—what can you do to rekindle her love for you and your love for her?

Marriage

Be subject to one another out of reverence for Christ.

Ephesians 5:21 RSV

Wives, submit to your husbands as to the Lord.
Ephesians 5:22

And you husbands must love your wives with the same love Christ showed the church. He gave up his life for her.

Ephesians 5:25 NLT

As the Scriptures say, "A man leaves his father and mother to get married, and he becomes like one person with his wife."

Ephesians 5:31 CEV

Age Before Beauty

From German pastor and theologian Helmut Thielicke comes this beautiful picture of a marriage where love has continued to grow all through the years:

"I once knew a very old married couple who radiated a profound happiness. The wife, especially, who was almost unable to move because of her age and illness, possessed a kind face etched with a hundred lines by the joys and sufferings of many years. She exhibited such a gratitude for life that I was touched to the quick.

"I asked myself what could possibly be the source of this kindly person's radiance. In so many respects they were quite ordinary people, and their home indicated only the most modest comforts.

"Suddenly I saw where it all came from. I saw these two speaking to each other, and their eyes hanging upon each other. It became clear to me that this woman was dearly loved.

"It was not that she was loved all those years by her husband because she was a cheerful and pleasant person. It was the other way around. Because she was so loved, she became the person I saw before me."

In your marriage, you can enjoy a lifelong relationship with your beloved. "Because she is so loved" by you.

Mercy

Surely goodness and mercy shall follow me All the days of my life; And I will dwell in the house of the LORD forever.

Psalm 23:6 NKJV

Please, Lord, remember, you have always been patient and kind.

Psalm 25:6 CEV

Mercy and truth are met together; righteousness and peace have kissed each other.

Psalm 85:10 KJV

For I desired mercy, and not sacrifice; and the knowledge of God more than burnt offerings.

Hosea 6:6 KJV

The Quality of Mercy

Outside the Bible, few treasures are worth memorizing and taking to heart than these words of Shakespeare depicting mercy:

The quality of mercy is not strain'd
It droppeth as the gentle rain from heaven
Upon the place beneath: It is twice blest.
It blesseth him that gives and him that takes:
'Tis mightiest in the mightiest: it becomes
The throned monarch better than its crown;
His sceptre shows the force of temporal power;
The attribute to awe and majesty,
Wherein doth sit the dread and fear of kings;
But mercy is above this sceptred sway;
It is enthroned in the hearts of kings;
It is an attribute to God Himself;
And earthly power doth then show likest God's
When mercy seasons justice.

Mercy

Blessed are the merciful, for they will be shown mercy.

Matthew 5:7

Woe to you, scribes and Pharisees, hypocrites! For you pay tithe of mint and anise and cummin, and have neglected the weightier matters of the law: justice and mercy and faith. These you ought to have done, without leaving the others undone.

Matthew 23:23 NKJV

But God was merciful! We were dead because of our sins, but God loved us so much that he made us alive with Christ and God's wonderful kindness is what saves you.

Ephesians 2:4-5 CEV

This is a true saying, and everyone should believe it: Christ Jesus came into the world to save sinners—and I was the worst of them all. But that is why God had mercy on me, so that Christ Jesus could use me as a prime example of his great patience with even the worst sinners. Then others will realize that they, too, can believe in him and receive eternal life.

1 Timothy 1:15-16 NLT

The Merciful Shall Obtain Mercy

Thomas Barnardo is all but forgotten today, but he is one of the great Christian heroes of the 1800s.

He spent his life working among the poor and homeless in London's East End. He built a home for destitute children that housed 400 boys and girls. He bought the Edinburgh Castle Gin Palace and turned it into a center for evangelistic and alcoholism-prevention activities. He built Girls Village, which served more than 9,000 girls. In all, more than 60,000 children benefited from the centers and homes he built.

Some of Barnardo's activities, however, were quite controversial. In extreme cases where he found children being cruelly abused by their parents or guardians, he would actually "abduct" them—a practice clearly against the law. Barnardo felt bound by a higher law, however, even though it made him subject to criminal charges and bitter custody battles.

Eventually, the laws were changed to protect children, so Barnardo's illegal actions no longer became necessary. Chief among those responsible for the legal changes: lawyers, doctors, business leaders, military officers, academicians, and ministers of state who once had been destitute before being rescued by Thomas Barnardo.

These to whom Barnardo had showed mercy helped change the laws so the laws became merciful to him.

Obedience

Jesus answered him, "If a man loves me, he will keep my word, and my Father will love him, and we will come to him and make our home with him."

John 14:23 RSV

With these weapons we break down every proud argument that keeps people from knowing God. With these weapons we conquer their rebellious ideas, and we teach them to obey Christ.

2 Corinthians 10:5 NLT

Jesus is God's own Son, but still he had to suffer before he could learn what it really means to obey God. Suffering made Jesus perfect, and now he can save forever all who obey him.

Hebrews 5:8-9 CEV

That is why I am suffering as I am. Yet I am not ashamed, because I know whom I have believed, and am convinced that he is able to guard what I have entrusted to him for that day.

2 Timothy 1:12

Knowing When It's Okay to Steal

Earl Weaver, former manager of the Baltimore Orioles, had a rule that no player could steal a base unless he gave the steal sign. This ruling upset Reggie Jackson, who felt he knew the pitchers and catchers well enough to judge when he could steal. One day he decided to steal without a sign. He easily beat the throw to second base. As he shook the dirt from his uniform, he smiled with delight, feeling he had vindicated his judgment.

Weaver became enraged and pulled Jackson from the game for a pinch runner. He ordered Jackson to sit next to him and watch what happened next:

- The next batter was Lee May, a major power hitter. Because first base was open, the opposing team intentionally walked May.
- The batter after May had a poor average against this pitcher, so Weaver had to send in a pinch-hitter, weakening his bench strength.

Jackson got the point. He had seen a stolen base only as a test of his talent. Weaver viewed it as part of his overall strategy.

Obedience is not restricted to children. Even adults must resist the temptation to place their own shortsighted interests ahead of the big picture.

Obedience

Jesus answered, "My teaching is not my own. It comes from him who sent me. If anyone chooses to do God's will he will find out whether my teaching comes from God or whether I speak on my own. He who speaks on his own does so to gain honor for himself, but he who works for the honor of the one who sent him is a man of truth; there is nothing false about him."

John 7:16-18

Then Jesus said to those Jews who believed Him, "If you abide in My word, you are My disciples indeed. And you shall know the truth, and the truth shall make you free."

John 8:31-32 NKJV

For a shepherd enters through the gate. The gatekeeper opens the gate for him, and the sheep hear his voice and come to him. He calls his own sheep by name and leads them out. After he has gathered his own flock, he walks ahead of them, and they follow him because they recognize his voice.

John 10:2-4 NLT

By this my Father is glorified, that you bear much fruit, and so prove to be my disciples. As the Father has loved me, so have I loved you; abide in my love.

John 15:8-9 RSV

Resisting the Ruts

Sometimes, obedience is a question of which voice to obey.

A biologist once placed several caterpillars on the rim of a pot that held a delicious (to a caterpillar) green plant. He lined them up head-to-tail with no break in the circular parade.

The tiny creatures walked around the rim of the pot for days until they died of exhaustion and starvation. Food was only inches away, but the follow-the-leader instinct was even stronger than the drive to eat and survive.

People sometimes find themselves in situations like this. When it happens, we can ask ourselves three questions:

1. *Who am I following?* We adopt certain patterns in our lives because someone has taught them to us directly or by example. It's important to choose a wise leader to follow.

2. *Is this rut of my own making?* It's common to choose a rut because it's comfortable and avoids risk. If all else fails, choose a new rut!

3. *Where does this rut lead?* Ruts develop when we lose a sense of vision for our lives. Developing new goals will take us out of our ruts.

To resist the ruts in your life, obey the still, small voice within!

Patience

My brethren, count it all joy when ye fall into
divers temptations; Knowing this, that the trying
of your faith worketh patience. But let patience
have her perfect work, that ye may be perfect and
entire, wanting nothing.

James 1:2-4 KJV

This you know, my beloved brethren. But let
every one be quick to hear, slow to speak and slow
to anger.

James 1:19 NASB

Dear brothers and sisters, you must be patient as
you wait for the Lord's return. Consider the
farmers who eagerly look for the rains in the fall
and in the spring. They patiently wait for the
precious harvest to ripen.

James 5:7-8 NLT

Brothers, as an example of patience in the face of
suffering, take the prophets who spoke in the
name of the Lord. As you know, we consider
blessed those who have persevered. You have
heard of Job's perseverance and have seen what
the Lord finally brought about. The Lord is full of
compassion and mercy.

James 5:10-11

Two-Minute Drills

Most Americans hear "Montana" and think of two things: a state and a star.

Joe Montana has been a football great by any standards. Before his retirement he led the San Francisco 49ers to four Super Bowl victories. His stats for 16 seasons: 3,409 passes for 40,551 yards, 273 touchdowns, and the highest quarterback rating (92.3) of any passer in history.

A town in Montana changed its name to Joe. Teammates and opponents alike praised his grace and skill, especially his cool ability to run a two-minute drill for a come-from-behind win.

It wasn't always like that. He grew up in Monongahela, Pennsylvania, in the long shadows of gridiron greats like Unitas, Blanda, and Namath. In college, he was Notre Dame's seventh-string quarterback. Even though as a senior he led his team to victory in the 1979 Cotton Bowl, no NFL team sought him out. Finally he was chosen as the 82nd player named in the draft. He sat on the bench his rookie year, and got his chance only when the starting quarterback was injured.

As his career unfolded from high school to college, from the pros to the Super Bowl, and from a last-minute win to the Hall of Fame, Joe Montana's watchword has always been *patience*.

Patience

At the time I have decided, my words will come true. You can trust what I say about the future. It may take a long time, but keep on waiting—it will happen!

Habakkuk 2:3 CEV

For you have need of endurance, so that after you have done the will of God, you may receive the promise: "For yet a little while, and He who is coming will come and will not tarry."

Hebrews 10:36-37 NKJV

Therefore, since we are surrounded by such a great cloud of witnesses, let us throw off everything that hinders and the sin that so easily entangles, and let us run with perseverance the race marked out for us.

Hebrews 12:1

So make every effort to apply the benefits of these promises to your life. Then your faith will produce a life of moral excellence. A life of moral excellence leads to knowing God better. Knowing God leads to self-control. Self-control leads to patient endurance, and patient endurance leads to godliness.

2 Peter 1:5-6 NLT

Waiting for the Long Arm

After losing by just one vote in the 1993 mayoral election in Hickory, Mississippi, Charlie Lewis retired to Michigan. He was seventy-two years old. He believed his election challenge was unlikely to succeed in the courts, and so he decided to enjoy the quiet life.

Then came an unexpected phone call. Return at once to Mississippi, his attorney urged. The state's Supreme Court had thrown out three absentee ballots cast for the incumbent mayor, wiping out his one vote victory.

"I'd almost forgotten about it," Lewis said in response to the news. "It's been more than two years, and when you get to be seventy-two years old, I guess you learn how to digest things."

Still, he returned to his hometown and to the opportunities to do good that awaited him.

Charlie Lewis became the first black mayor of the tiny town of 500 nestled in the red clay hills of east Mississippi. "I waited quite awhile," he was quoted as saying on his first day, "but the law takes a long time."

Martin Luther King often preached that "the arm of the universe is long, but it bends toward justice." When discouraged, remember this promise: Through patience you, too, can receive the embrace of that long arm.

Peace

And he will judge between the nations, And will render decisions for many peoples; And they will hammer their swords into plowshares, and their spears into pruning hooks. Nation will not lift up sword against nation, And never again will they learn war.

Isaiah 2:4 NASB

Open the gates, that the righteous nation which keeps faith may enter in. Thou dost keep him in perfect peace, whose mind is stayed on thee, because he trusts in thee.

Isaiah 26:2-3 RSV

And this righteousness will bring peace. Quietness and confidence will fill the land forever.

Isaiah 32:17 NLT

For thus saith the LORD, Behold, I will extend peace to her like a river, and the glory of the Gentiles like a flowing stream: then shall ye suck, ye shall be borne upon her sides, and be dandled upon her knees.

Isaiah 66:12 KJV

Risking Your Life for Peace

While he was a pastor in Indianapolis, Henry Ward Beecher preached a series of sermons about gambling and drunkenness. He soundly denounced the men of the community who profited from these sins.

The next week, while Beecher was out for a walk, a man jumped out in front of him and pulled out a gun. He demanded that Beecher retract what he had said the previous Sunday.

"Take it back right here!" he demanded. Swearing at Beecher, he threatened him, "If you don't, I'll shoot you on the spot!"

Beecher calmly replied, "Shoot away!" The man was so taken aback by his response that he turned around and slunk away. As Beecher resumed his walk and left the scene, he called out over his shoulder, "I don't believe you can hit the mark as well as I did."

Peace involves more than the cessation of tensions. It requires active engagement with life, not a passive acceptance of the status quo. Sometimes peace may put us into a life and death situation where our convictions about violence will be put to the test. Today you may be challenged to speak up, speak out, and stand up for your beliefs. How will you respond?

Peace

For to us a child is born, to us a son is given, and the government will be on his shoulders. And he will be called Wonderful Counselor, Mighty God, Everlasting Father, Prince of Peace. Of the increase of his government and peace there will be no end.

Isaiah 9:6-7

Blessed are the peacemakers, for they shall be called sons of God.

Matthew 5:9 NKJV

Suddenly many other angels came down from heaven and joined in praising God. They said: "Praise God in heaven! Peace on earth to everyone who pleases God."

Luke 2:13-14 CEV

But the wisdom that comes from heaven is first of all pure. It is also peace loving, gentle at all times, and willing to yield to others. It is full of mercy and good deeds. It shows no partiality and is always sincere.

James 3:17 NLT

The Miraculous Bombshells

During a run over Kassel, Germany, Elmer Bendiner's B-17 bomber took a barrage of flack from Nazi anti-aircraft. He could feel the plane being hit, yet he and his crew returned to base after a successful mission.

Bendiner was even more amazed when he was told that a 20-millimeter shell pierced the fuel tank but did not cause an explosion. He started to ask the crew chief for the shell as a souvenir of their unbelievable luck. But the crew chief told him that not just one shell had been found in the gas tanks, but eleven! Eleven unexploded shells? It truly seemed to be a miracle.

The shells were sent to the armorers to be defused, after which intelligence officers came by to retrieve them. The armorers reported something even more mystifying—when they opened the shells, they found no explosive charge in any of them. They appeared to be empty and harmless.

One of the shells, however, was not completely empty. It contained a carefully rolled piece of paper. On it was scrawled a message in the Czech language of a prison camp worker:

This is all we can do for you now.

It was a miracle, all right, not of misfired shells, but of peace-loving hearts.

Persecution

I say: Love your enemies! Pray for those who persecute you! In that way you will be acting as true sons of your Father in heaven.

Matthew 5:44-45 TLB

Bless them which persecute you: bless, and curse not.

Romans 12:14 KJV

Love your enemies, and be good to everyone who hates you. Ask God to bless anyone who curses you, and pray for everyone who is cruel to you.

Luke 6:27-28 CEV

If your enemy is hungry, give him food to eat; And if he is thirsty, give him water to drink; For you will heap burning coals on his head, And the LORD will reward you.

Proverbs 25:21-22 NASB

The Worst Persecution: Giving Up

Paul the Apostle wrote many of his epistles, which have influenced the growth of Christianity more than any other writings, while in prison awaiting trial.

Christopher Columbus faced constant grumbling and near mutiny during his initial voyage to the Western Hemisphere.

Sir Walter Raleigh wrote *The History of the World* during a thirteen-year imprisonment.

Martin Luther translated the Bible from Latin into the language of the German people while under house arrest at the Wartburg Castle.

Dante wrote the *Divine Comedy* during twenty years in exile.

John Bunyan wrote *Pilgrim's Progress* in a Bedford jail.

Beethoven composed some of his greatest music after becoming deaf.

John Milton wrote some of his most spiritual poems after going blind.

Martin Luther King Jr. wrote his most famous treatise against segregation from a cell in a Birmingham jail.

Mary Groda-Lewis endured sixteen years of illiteracy because of unrecognized dyslexia but finally graduated from college and medical school to become a leading researcher in the disease.

Many other great persons created some of their most important contributions while suffering persecution and oppression. In comparison to imprisonment and ridicule, however, the temptation to give up is the severest persecution of all.

Persecution

O LORD my God, in thee do I put my trust: save me from all them that persecute me, and deliver me.

Psalm 7:1 KJV

Whenever we are in need, we should come bravely before the throne of our merciful God. There we will be treated with undeserved kindness, and we will find help.

Hebrews 4:16 CEV

In fact, everyone who wants to live a godly life in Christ Jesus will be persecuted.

2 Timothy 3:12

Of course you know that such troubles are a part of God's plan for us Christians. Even while we were still with you we warned you ahead of time that suffering would soon come—and it did.

1 Thessalonians 3:3-4 TLB

Undeserved Tragedies

Joni Eareckson became paralyzed through a teenage diving accident. In the years since, she has become a much-loved speaker, singer, writer, and artist. Here is one reflection on the tragedy that struck her:

"What happened on July 30, 1967, was the beginning of an incredible adventure which I feel compelled to share because of what I have learned.

"If I were still on my feet, it's hard to say how things might have gone. I probably would have drifted through life—dissatisfied and disillusioned. When I was in high school, I reacted to life selfishly. I lived for the pleasure I wanted—and almost always at the expense of others.

"Oscar Wilde wrote, 'In this world there are only two tragedies. One is not getting what one wants, and the other is getting it.' To rephrase this thought, I suggest there are likewise only two joys. One is having God answer all your prayers; the other is not receiving the answer to all your prayers. I believe this because I have found that God knows my needs infinitely better than I know them."

When nothing seems to be going the way you want, consider the possibility that God is blessing you through the way things are going.

Perseverance

We gladly suffer, because we know that suffering helps us to endure. And endurance builds character, which gives us a hope that will never disappoint us. All of this happens because God has given us the Holy Spirit, who fills our hearts with his love.

Romans 5:3-5 CEV

[Love] always protects, always trusts, always hopes, always perseveres.

1 Corinthians 13:7

Blessed is the man who endures trial, for when he has stood the test he will receive the crown of life which God has promised to those who love him.

James 1:12 RSV

May the Lord direct your hearts into God's love and Christ's perseverance.

2 Thessalonians 3:5

An Oath of Perseverance

1. I will never give up so long as I know I'm right.

2. I will believe that all things will work out for me if I hang on until the end.

3. I will be courageous and undismayed in the face of odds.

4. I will not permit anyone to intimidate me or deter me from my goals.

5. I will fight to overcome all physical limitations and setbacks.

6. I will try again and again and yet again to accomplish my dreams.

7. I will take new faith and resolution from the knowledge that all successful people have had to overcome defeat and adversity.

8. I will never surrender to discouragement or despair, no matter what.

—Herman Sherman

Recite these vows every morning. Keep them with you and review them when you're stuck in traffic, trapped in a tense meeting, tossing and turning at night, preparing to meet a deadline, or sitting down for a serious talk with your child.

Perseverance

You need to persevere so that when you have done the will of God, you will receive what he has promised.

Hebrews 10:36

The good soil represents honest, good-hearted people who hear God's message, cling to it, and steadily produce a huge harvest.

Luke 8:15 NLT

You know that you learn to endure by having your faith tested. But you must learn to endure everything, so that you will be completely mature and not lacking in anything.

James 1:3-4 CEV

Be of good courage, and he shall strengthen your heart, all ye that hope in the LORD.

Psalm 31:24 KJV

Never Give Up on Your Dreams

Jerry Richardson faced an important decision in 1961. As a wide receiver for the Baltimore Colts, his job was high paying and glamorous. Then he was turned down for a raise he had requested—for only $250 a year. Rather than accept the disappointment, he decided the time had come to move on to his next dream: to start his own business.

Richardson moved his family back to his hometown in South Carolina, where he invested in a new fast-food restaurant, buying the first Hardee's franchise in America.

He went from catching passes on Sundays to flipping burgers twelve hours a day. After hours he cleaned stoves and scrubbed floors. His reward? $417 a month the first year.

Richardson refused to punt. He applied his gridiron discipline to produce sizzling results on his griddles. He turned his locker-room enthusiasm into the friendliest service in town. Before long, business boomed.

Today Jerry Richardson heads one of the America's largest food-service companies, with annual sales of $3.7 billion. Now he's investing some of his profits in his next dream: ownership of the NFL's Carolina Panthers.

Perseverance is more than doing the same thing over and over. It's applying what you know in new and successful ways.

Priorities

Lo, children are an heritage of the LORD: and the fruit of the womb is his reward. As arrows are in the hand of a mighty man; so are children of the youth.

Psalm 127:3-4 KJV

Trust in the LORD with all your heart; do not depend on your own understanding. Seek his will in all you do, and he will direct your paths.

Proverbs 3:5-6 NLT

This is what the LORD says: "Stand at the crossroads and look; ask for the ancient paths, ask where the good way is, and walk in it, and you will find rest for your souls."

Jeremiah 6:16

Fathers, do not provoke your children, lest they become discouraged.

Colossians 3:21 RSV

Growing Up

As a professional pilot, Jim's job required a lot of time away from home. After every long trip his wife and four kids would meet him at the door with loving hugs and kisses.

After one joyful reunion, he picked up his youngest, and asked, "What do you want to be when you grow up?" The child responded without hesitation, "A pilot."

He smiled approvingly and asked, "Why a pilot?" His little daughter looked sadly at him and replied, "So I can spend more time with you."

Not long afterward, Jim took a position that gave him more time at home.

Most families struggle with this tension between work and home It's hard to balance the priorities, since both are important. Experts are coming to a consensus, however, that both work and home flourish better if we spend the first twenty years or so giving our children the highest priority. Those who do, these experts say, earn just as much in their last twenty years as do those who give all their energy to their careers.

There are some things you learn about life from your children that you simply can't learn from your boss. Now that's what growing up is all about!

Priorities

Memorize his laws and tell them to your children over and over again. Talk about them all the time, whether you're at home or walking along the road or going to bed at night, or getting up in the morning.

Deuteronomy 6:6-7 CEV

He will give you all you need from day to day if you live for him and make the Kingdom of God your primary concern.

Matthew 6:33 NLT

People of Israel, what does the Lord your God want from you? The Lord wants you to respect and follow him, to love and serve him with all your heart and soul, and to obey his laws and teachings that I am giving you today. Do this, and all will go well for you.

Deuteronomy 10:12-13 CEV

Decide today whom you will obey . . . As for me and my family, we will serve the Lord.

Joshua 24:15 TLB

Kids, Let Me Introduce You to the Sky

When John was a boy, his immigrant father took his family on a journey across the American continent. It took the family a full year to make their way from coast to coast.

As each sunset and sunrise glorified the heavens, the Scotsman would take his children out to introduce them to the sky. He would point out the different cloud formations and describe them as different styles of "the robes of God."

When he grew up, John never forgot this family trip of a lifetime. In fact, John Muir became one of America's greatest naturalists. Through his influence, many of our national parks were established, so that millions of families now can enjoy majestic mountains, glacial meadows, redwood forests, awesome canyons . . . and glorious skies above them all. The lovely Muir Woods in northern California honor his name.

John Muir's father practiced the most important form of stewardship—he invested in his children. He pointed them to great possibilities. Certainly the family could not afford to be without income for an entire year. On the other hand, what father can afford not to invest time teaching a child to search the sky? The returns on such an investment are immeasurable.

Rejection

You have been my helper. Do not reject me or forsake me, O God my Savior. Though my father and mother forsake me, the LORD will receive me.
Psalm 27:9-10

[Jesus said]: "Those the Father has given me will come to me, and I will never reject them."
John 6:37 NLT

Everyone who honors your name can trust you, because you are faithful to all who depend on you.
Psalm 9:10 CEV

He who rejects this instruction does not reject man but God, who gives you his Holy Spirit.
1 Thessalonians 4:8

Turning Rejection into Opportunity

Ernie was just out of school, eager to start his newspaper career, but kept encountering rejection because of the age-old dilemma—he couldn't get a job because he lacked experience, and he couldn't get experience without a job.

He saw a classified ad for a position, which said applicants would be interviewed at 10 a.m. the next day. He worked all night to make his resume look as promising as possible and prepared a portfolio of his writing samples.

Arriving early the next morning, he was stunned to see a long line. He took his place at the end and recognized several competitors as older, more experienced reporters.

Ernie had an idea. He wrote a note, and took it to the editor's secretary, telling her it was extremely important to show it to her boss immediately.

When the editor read the note, he hurried through the rest of the interviews. It said, "Dear Sir, I'm the young man who is tenth in line. Please don't make any decisions until you see me."

This kind of resourcefulness and refusal to take no for an answer was just what the editor was looking for in a reporter. Ernie had turned rejection into opportunity.

Rejection

He was hated and rejected; his life was filled with sorrow and terrible suffering. No one wanted to look at him. We despised him and said, "He is a nobody!"

Isaiah 53:3 CEV

The LORD will not forsake His people, for His great name's sake, because it has pleased the LORD to make you His people.

1 Samuel 12:22 NKJV

God will not reject a man of integrity, Nor will He support the evildoers.

Job 8:20 NASB

The LORD your God goes with you; he will never leave you nor forsake you.

Deuteronomy 31:6

How Your Enemies Help You Grow

The fact that others reject you proves nothing.

It's said that General Robert E. Lee was asked by Confederate President Jefferson Davis to give his opinion about a certain officer. Lee gave a glowing report.

One who overheard was greatly astonished at Lee's words and said to him, "General, do you not know that the man of whom you speak so highly to the President is one of your bitterest enemies, and misses no opportunity to malign you?"

"Yes," said Lee, "but the President asked my opinion of him; he did not ask for the man's opinion of me."

When you speak well of your adversaries, you grow in three ways:

- First, you strengthen your own character. You learn to rise above cheap criticism.
- Second, you defuse your opponent's attack. Anyone who hears both your praise and your enemy's disdain will hold a more favorable opinion of you than of him.
- Third, you improve in the hard work of living at peace with others. It takes very little effort or intelligence to criticize; but finding something good to say about a critic requires some diligence.

An enemy's criticism provides an opportunity for you to grow and gain respect.

Restoration

Restore to me the joy of thy salvation, and uphold me with a willing spirit . . . The sacrifice acceptable to God is a broken spirit; a broken and contrite heart, O God, thou wilt not despise.

Psalm 51:12,17 RSV

And the God of all grace, who called you to his eternal glory in Christ, after you have suffered a little while, will himself restore you and make you strong, firm and steadfast. To him be the power for ever and ever. Amen.

1 Peter 5:10-11

You let me rest in fields of green grass. You lead me to streams of peaceful water, and you refresh my life. You are true to your name, and you lead me along the right paths.

Psalm 23:2-3 CEV

Turn us back to You, O Lord, and we will be restored; renew our days as of old.

Lamentations 5:21 NKJV

J. C. Penney's Greatest Store

J. C. Penney worked many years to become a financial success before a crisis changed his life.

"When I worked for six dollars a week at Joslin's Dry Goods Store back in Denver," he recalled, "it was my ambition to be worth one hundred thousand dollars. When I reached that goal, I felt a certain temporary satisfaction, but it soon wore off, and my sights were set on becoming worth a million dollars."

Penney and his wife worked hard to expand the business—so hard that one day Mrs. Penney became ill and developed pneumonia, which claimed her life.

"When she died," he said, "my world crashed about me. What had money meant to my wife? I felt mocked by life, even by God Himself."

Several more fiery trials ensued, and soon J. C. Penney was financially ruined and in deep emotional distress. At this point, he began to acknowledge his self-centered nature and his idolatry of money, and he experienced a spiritual conversion.

"When I was brought to humility and the knowledge of dependence on God, it was forthcoming, and a light illumined my being."

$100,000. $1,000,000. The death of a loved one. Sometimes it takes tragedy, not success, to restore us to the divine image in which we were created.

Restoration

Repent ye therefore, and be converted, that your sins may be blotted out, when the times of refreshing shall come from the presence of the Lord.

Acts 3:19 KJV

Restore us, O God; make your face shine upon us, that we may be saved.

Psalm 80:3

Cast away from you all your transgressions, whereby ye have transgressed; and make you a new heart and a new spirit.

Ezekiel 18:31 KJV

So turn to God! Give up your sins, and you will be forgiven. Then that time will come when the Lord will give you fresh strength.

Acts 3:19-20 CEV

Deciding When To Be Disturbed

A young family was moving to a new house. On moving day, Joe announced that an important meeting had been called at his new job, and he would be unable to help. Consequently, Jean had to handle the move by herself.

After the moving van came and left, Jean found herself standing in the living room surrounded by boxes to be unpacked, appliances to be hooked up, a screaming baby and a five-year-old who decided to throw a metal toy truck through the picture window.

Fortunately nobody was hurt, but jagged glass fell everywhere and a gale-force wind blew through the house. Jean felt she had to call Joe and tell him what had happened.

Joe's secretary informed her that he was in a meeting and couldn't be disturbed. "May I take a message?" the secretary asked. "No, that's okay," Jean said, knowing Joe was notoriously lax about returning her calls. "Wait," Jean said, "Just tell him the insurance will cover everything."

The instant Joe got the message he called home.

It's wonderful to know God's forgiving love restores us, just as insurance restored the broken window. God never says, "I can't be disturbed" when we call on Him. May we treat our families with the same spirit.

Self-Control

Follow the Lord's rules for doing his work, just as an athlete either follows the rules or is disqualified and wins no prize.

2 Timothy 2:5 TLB

Knowing God leads to self-control. Self-control leads to patient endurance, and patient endurance leads to godliness.

2 Peter 1:6 NLT

Those who belong to Christ Jesus have nailed the passions and desires of their sinful nature to his cross.

Galatians 5:24 NLT

Clothe yourselves with the Lord Jesus Christ, and do not think about how to gratify the desires of the sinful nature.

Romans 13:14

Keep Your Eyes on Your Prize

Henry Ford worked long hours in a little brick building behind his home, building the prototype for what would become the first Ford automobile. Enthusiasm and excitement fueled him, and he had to make himself stop to eat and sleep.

Then, even before he had completed this first model, Ford starting thinking of ways to improve it. The thrill of what he was working on began to wane—why spend all this time finishing a car that's already inferior?

Something inside him compelled him to press on, as if he sensed he must focus his total energy on the first car and finish what he started. His concentration was rewarded—as he finished his original dream, he learned many new lessons about design and construction which he later applied to the second car.

As a result, Henry Ford discovered a most important secret about life and work: The more completely you are able to focus on your present task, the more creatively you can envision future ones.

How often we come home exhausted and distracted, unable to find the energy our families require. The secret: Learn to be fully present in this moment, and let the next moment take care of itself.

Self-Control

Set a watch, O Lord, before my mouth; keep the door of my lips. Incline not my heart to any evil thing.

Psalm 141:3-4 KJV

Do not let any unwholesome talk come out of your mouths, but only what is helpful for building others up according to their needs, that it may benefit those who listen.

Ephesians 4:29

Young people can live a clean life by obeying your word.

Psalm 119:9 CEV

I urge you therefore, brethren, by the mercies of God, to present your bodies a living and holy sacrifice, acceptable to God, which is your spiritual service of worship.

Romans 12:1 NASB

Timing Is Everything

Three brawny, rough-looking fellows on huge, roaring motorcycles pulled over and parked in front of the highway cafe. They came in and sat at the counter alongside a meek little guy who was reading his paper.

While waiting to order their meals, one of the toughs reached over and took a drink out of the little guy's coffee, then sneered at him, daring him to do anything about it. The little guy kept reading his paper. The second picked up a fork and speared the man's pork chop and devoured it. The third took a handful of salad and downed it in one bite, and all the while the little guy minded his own business.

Finally, with no food to eat, he got up, paid his bill, and walked out.

One of the three bullies, unhappy that they hadn't succeeded in provoking the little guy, commented to the waitress, "Boy, he sure ain't much of a fighter, is he?"

"Well, I guess not," the waitress replied. Then, looking out the window, she added, "I guess he's not much of a truck driver, either. He just ran over three motorcycles."

Self-control is a matter of learning exactly when and where and how to lose control.

Shame

Do your best to present yourself to God as one approved, a workman who does not need to be ashamed and who correctly handles the word of truth.

2 Timothy 2:15

We don't do shameful things that must be kept secret. And we don't try to fool anyone or twist God's message around. God is our witness that we speak only the truth, so others will be sure that we can be trusted.

2 Corinthians 4:2 CEV

May those who hope in you not be disgraced because of me, O Lord, the Lord Almighty; may those who seek you not be put to shame.

Psalm 69:6

Behold, I am laying in Zion a stone that will make men stumble, a rock that will make them fall; and he who believes in him will not be put to shame.

Romans 9:33 RSV

Finding Flair in Your Flaws

When we find ourselves feeling ashamed of a flaw in ourselves, it's wise to remember this story:

A king once owned a valuable diamond, one of the rarest and most perfect in the world. One day he dropped the diamond, and a deep scratch marred its face. The king summoned the best jewel experts in the land to remove the blemish, but all agreed the only way to remove the scratch was to cut away a part of the surface, reducing its weight and value.

Finally, one expert appeared and assured the king he could repair the diamond and actually increase its worth. His self-confidence was convincing, and the king authorized the artisan to go to work.

In a few days, he returned the diamond. The king was amazed to find that the diamond now was etched with a tiny, lovely rose. On closer examination he discovered that the former scratch had become the stem of this exquisite flower. Now, no more beautiful diamond existed anywhere in the world.

Our children often feel shame when others make fun of a physical difference. As fathers, we can assure them that God can transform any blemish into a thing of beauty.

Shame

Then, when that happens, we are able to hold our heads high no matter what happens and know that all is well, for we know how dearly God loves us, and we feel this warm love everywhere within us because God has given us the Holy Spirit to fill our hearts with his love.

Romans 5:5 TLB

Therefore being justified by faith, we have peace with God through our Lord Jesus Christ.

Romans 5:1 KJV

Fear not; you will no longer live in shame. The shame of your youth and the sorrows of widowhood will be remembered no more.

Isaiah 54:4 NLT

No one whose hope is in you will ever be put to shame, but they will be put to shame who are treacherous without excuse.

Psalm 25:3

Don't Be Ashamed to Have a Bad Day

On a bleak midwinter morning, Jim felt overwhelmed with a sense of failure. He had lost his job, again. Alcohol had wreaked havoc on his life and although he had been without a drink for some months and was involved in Alcoholics Anonymous, on this day he could see no future for himself.

The image of the shotgun in the attic began to fill his thoughts. Finally, he aroused himself and said, "I'll go see Ted."

Ted was his AA sponsor, a crusty, straight-talking farmer. When Jim arrived, he found Ted sitting by his wood-burning stove. They began to talk together, and Ted told Jim things weren't going well on the farm. They spent nearly two hours, stoking the fire and comparing notes.

On the way home, Jim thought to himself, *At least I've made it through the day.*

A few days later Jim attended his next AA meeting, and saw Ted again. During the meeting, Ted stood up.

"A week ago," Ted began, his lip trembling, "my life seemed hopeless. My farm was in terrible trouble. Then another recovering alcoholic stopped by and cheered me up and gave me a reason to keep going."

When a problem makes you feel ashamed, remember, God can use your problem to answer somebody else's need.

Speech

Hard work is worthwhile, but empty talk will make you poor.

Proverbs 14:23 CEV

The kingdom of God does not consist in words, but in power.

1 Corinthians 4:20 NASB

If I speak in the tongues of men and of angels, but have not love, I am only a resounding gong or a clanging cymbal.

1 Corinthians 13:1

Let your speech always be gracious, seasoned with salt, so that you may know how you ought to answer every one.

Colossians 4:6 RSV

How To Make a Great Speech

When reporters bombarded Cardinal Francis Spellman with questions during a surprise interview, he finally pointed to a mounted fish on the wall behind his desk, which bore this plaque:

If I had kept my mouth shut, I wouldn't be here.

Perhaps the most important speeches we'll ever make come down to the simple words "Yes" or "No"—without excuses, without explanations. Most of our crucial decisions eventually come to this.

To reach the point of answering Yes or No, we can meditate on these three core questions:

1. *Who besides me has to have a part in this decision?* If I am either the sole decision-maker or the one with the final say, I'm the one who must make the decision.

2. *What happens if I wait longer to decide?* In most cases, other people will be affected for better or worse. I must weigh my decision in the balances, trying to locate where on the fulcrum the weight of the argument tilts.

3. *Does the decision have a moral dimension?* If so, I may need to make an unpopular decision in order to hold onto my values.

All it takes to be a great speech maker is to master your Yes's and No's.

Speech

The mouth of the righteous man utters wisdom,
and his tongue speaks what is just.

Psalm 37:30

All Thy works shall give thanks to Thee, O LORD,
And Thy godly ones shall bless Thee. They shall
speak of the glory of Thy kingdom, And talk of
Thy power.

Psalm 145:10-11 NASB

It sounds strange for a fool to talk sensibly, but
it's even worse for a ruler to tell lies.

Proverbs 17:7 CEV

My message and my preaching were not with wise
and persuasive words, but with a demonstration of
the Spirit's power, so that your faith might not
rest on men's wisdom, but on God's power.

1 Corinthians 2:4-5

Giving Hearers Your Words' Worth

When Franklin D. Roosevelt was a young lawyer just getting started in New York, he was retained to handle a difficult civil case. The opposing attorney was a very experienced and effective trial lawyer. He completely outshone young Roosevelt in his final argument. However, becoming more and more full of himself, he orated on and on for several hours. Roosevelt noticed that the jury was finding it harder and harder to pay attention.

By the time Roosevelt stood up to speak, the jury was half asleep. Playing a hunch, he said to the jury:

"During this trial you have heard both sides present evidence. You have also listened to my distinguished colleague, a brilliant orator as you see.

"Here is my challenge to you: If you believe him and disbelieve the evidence, you must decide in his favor." With that, Roosevelt took his seat.

The jury was out only a few minutes and returned a verdict for Roosevelt's client.

It's not necessary to become a great orator in order to be persuasive. If you develop a command of the facts, and a respect for the truth, and an awareness of your own human nature, people will listen to you, understand you, and believe you.

Stewardship

And he sat down opposite the treasury, and watched the multitude putting money into the treasury. Many rich people put in large sums. And a poor widow came, and put in two copper coins, which make a penny. And he called his disciples to him, and said to them, "Truly, I say to you, this poor widow has put in more than all those who are contributing to the treasury."

Mark 12:41-43 RSV

Command those who are rich in this present world not to be arrogant nor to put their hope in wealth, which is so uncertain, but to put their hope in God, who richly provides us with everything for our enjoyment. Command them to do good, to be rich in good deeds, and to be generous and willing to share.

1 Timothy 6:17-18

Although they were going through hard times and were very poor, they were glad to give generously. They gave as much as they could afford and even more, simply because they wanted to.

2 Corinthians 8:2-3 CEV

On every Lord's Day, each of you should put aside some amount of money in relation to what you have earned and save it for this offering. Don't wait until I get there and then try to collect it all at once.

1 Corinthians 16:2 NLT

Turning Pennies into Fortunes

Some years ago in Philadelphia, fifty-seven pennies were found under a little girl's pillow, pennies that left an unforgettable mark on the city.

The little girl attended what was called the Temple Sunday School. She, like many other children, joined their parents in supporting the expansion of the facilities by saving their pennies. Two years after she started her savings, the little girl became ill and died. Shortly after her death, her parents found a small purse under her pillow, with fifty-seven pennies and a piece of paper with the following delicately handwritten note: "To help build the Temple bigger, so more children can go to Sunday School."

The pastor told the story to the congregation, and the local newspaper featured it, and soon her story had spread across the country. Soon the pennies grew into dollars, and the dollars into a huge fortune. The outcome can be seen in Philadelphia today.

There is a church that will seat 3,000 persons. And Temple University is home to thousands of students, including famous alumnus Bill Cosby. And Temple Hospital. And, yes, Temple Sunday School.

This is how stewardship works: Because one little girl gave what she could, millions were inspired to "go and do likewise."

Stewardship

The Lord answered, "Who then is the faithful and wise manager, whom the master puts in charge of his servants to give them their food allowance at the proper time? It will be good for that servant whom the master finds doing so when he returns."

Luke 12:42-43

Now, a person who is put in charge as a manager must be faithful.

1 Corinthians 4:2 NLT

Each of you has been blessed with one of God's many wonderful gifts to be used in the service of others. So use your gift well.

1 Peter 4:10 CEV

Good will come to him who is generous and lends freely, who conducts his affairs with justice.

Psalm 112:5

Stewardship Starts in the Heart

Here's how Oseola McCarty learned to practice stewardship.

She spent most of her life helping people look nice.

You see, she took in bundles of dirty clothes, and washed and ironed them. She started after having to drop out of school in the sixth grade, and carried out her work into her eighties.

Oseola never married, never had children. And for most of her eighty-seven years, Oseola McCarty spent almost no money. She lived in her old family home and wore simple clothes. She saved her money, most of it dollar bills and change, until she had amassed more than $150,000.

Then she made what people in Hattiesburg, Mississippi, are calling "The Gift." She donated her entire savings—all $150,000—to black college students across the state.

"I know it won't be too many years before I pass on," she explained, "and I wanted to share my wealth with the children."

Before her death, she was able to witness a number of "her children" graduate with the help of her financial support.

She teaches us all that stewardship starts in the heart, and when our hearts are full of love and gratitude, we'll find a way to leave a legacy.

Strength

I will love thee, O LORD, my strength.
Psalm 18:1 KJV

The Lord will give strength to His people; The Lord will bless His people with peace.
Psalm 29:11 NASB

God is wonderful and glorious. I pray that his Spirit will make you become strong followers and that Christ will live in your hearts because of your faith. Stand firm and be deeply rooted in his love.
Ephesians 3:16-17 CEV

I can do everything through him who gives me strength.
Philippians 4:13

Where True Strength Comes From

A house is just a house, until love comes in, transforming ordinary dust into angel dust.

Money has the power to pay for a house, but only love can furnish it with homey feelings.

Duty can make you pack a kid's lunch, but love inspires you to tuck a little note inside.

Keeping up can cause you to own a TV set, but love controls the remote.

Needing time alone can lead you to put the children to bed, but love tucks the covers in and reads a story.

Obligation can make you buy groceries, but love enhances a delicious meal with flowers and candles.

Compulsion keeps a sparkling house and manicured lawn, but love creates a play place inside and out.

Responsibility carries out the necessary tasks, but love enables you to do them for the sheer joy of service.

Duty can motivate you to call your faraway family members, but love frees you to prepare a care package full of their favorite things.

Yes, strength of will can keep things from falling into disrepair, but the power of love makes life worth living.

Strength

My flesh and my heart may fail, but God is the strength of my heart and my portion forever.
Psalm 73:26

You have armed me with strength for the battle; you have subdued my enemies under my feet.
2 Samuel 22:40 NLT

It is God that girdeth me with strength, and maketh my way perfect.
Psalm 18:32 KJV

The Lord gives strength to those who are weary.
Isaiah 40:29 CEV

Which Is Stronger, Rubber or Granite?

Before you answer, consider this:

When stonecutters engrave letters on a granite tombstone, they first coat the stone with a thin layer of rubber. They stencil the inscription onto the rubber, then cut the letters away to expose the granite. With a high-powered air pump, the stonecutter then blasts sand against the granite slab. Before long, the sand cuts into the granite and creates the etched letters. The areas covered with rubber are unaffected.

Stonecutters know that granite is hard and resistant. Rubber, in contrast, is light but flexible and absorbs the sandblasting shocks.

So it is with life—especially life with kids. Some dads are tough and unyielding and resist the normal rough-and-tumble of being a parent. This resistance is very tiring, and such parents often are irritable and exhausted. Others, however, realize that unpredictability and high energy are what growing up is all about, and they go with the flow of their kids' moods.

Next time you walk into a room where the noise and the energy are trying to sandblast your last ounce of strength, decide in that moment whether you're going to be a slab of granite, or a coat of rubber.

Stress

You will keep in perfect peace him whose mind is steadfast, because he trusts in you. Trust in the LORD forever, for the LORD, the LORD, is the Rock eternal.

Isaiah 26:3-4

The joy of the LORD is your strength.
Nehemiah 8:10 KJV

For unto us a child is born, unto us a son is given: and the government shall be upon his shoulder: and his name shall be called Wonderful, Counsellor, The mighty God, The everlasting Father, The Prince of Peace.

Isaiah 9:6 KJV

Make music for him on harps. Play beautiful melodies! Sound the trumpets and horns and celebrate with joyful songs for our LORD and King! Command the ocean to roar with all of its creatures, and the earth to shout with all of its people.

Psalm 98:5-7 CEV

Stress Is No Match for Joy

Handel's masterpiece, *The Messiah*, has inspired millions through the centuries. Few know, however, that George Frederick Handel composed the lengthy oratorio in approximately three weeks. The music literally "came to him" in a flurry of notes and motifs. He composed feverishly, as if driven by the unseen Composer to put pen to paper. It is also little known that Handel composed the work while his eyesight was failing. Or that he was facing the threat of debtor's prison because of large, outstanding bills.

Most people find it difficult to create under stress, especially when physical or financial problems are the root of that stress, and yet, Handel found a way.

He credits the completion of the work to one thing: *joy*. He was quoted as saying that he felt as if his heart would burst with joy at what he was hearing in his mind and heart. It was joy that compelled him to write, freed him to create, and ultimately found expression in the majestic "Hallelujah Chorus."

Handel lived to see his oratorio become a cherished tradition and a popular work. He was especially pleased to see it performed to raise money for benevolent causes—to help the less fortunate relieve the stress of life with joy.

Stress

Consider the blameless, observe the upright; there is a future for the man of peace.

Psalm 37:37

And the peace of God, which passeth all understanding, shall keep your hearts and minds through Christ Jesus.

Philippians 4:7 KJV

Come to Me, all you who labor and are heavy laden, and I will give you rest.

Matthew 11:28 NKJV

I tell you to love your enemies and pray for anyone who mistreats you.

Matthew 5:44 CEV

Love Lasers

Claire Townsend worked in one of our country's most stressful workplaces—a major motion picture studio. She came to dread the daily morning meetings. New owners had taken control of the studio, jobs were uncertain, and teamwork disappeared.

As she struggled with her stress, Claire paid more attention to her spiritual life. She began to pray again, and rediscovered the power of God's love. Even so, the morning meetings exhausted her.

Then during a particularly tense meeting, a thought came to her: *Pray, pray, pray. Do it now.* As she did so, she felt God's love pulsating within her then radiating out like sunlight. She aimed a "love laser" toward the person who was making her feel the worst. This co-worker suddenly got quiet, eyed her curiously, and Claire smiled back. One by one, she beamed God's love to each person around the table as she silently prayed.

Within minutes, the tone of the meeting completely changed. Compromise replaced confrontation. As the group relaxed, they became more creative and effective. From that day on, Claire looked forward to the meetings as an opportunity to share God's love.

Nobody needs to know if you pray to reduce stress next time you're in a tension-filled group, but you'll know, and God will know.

Success

It is very good if a man has received wealth from the Lord, and the good health to enjoy it. To enjoy your work and to accept your lot in life—that is indeed a gift from God.

Ecclesiastes 5:19 TLB

Riches and honor are with me, enduring wealth and prosperity. My fruit is better than gold, even fine gold, and my yield than choice silver.

Proverbs 8:18-19 RSV

Wealth and riches are in his house, and his righteousness endures forever.

Psalm 112:3

The mind of man plans his way, But the LORD directs his steps.

Proverbs 16:9 NASB

Opportunity Isn't Knocking, It's Waving at You

A young man trying to earn a living in his hometown of Kansas City was possessed of a burning desire to succeed as an illustrator. He approached every newspaper and magazine he knew of, trying to sell his cartoons. Each editor quickly and coldly turned him down, implying that he ought to try another line of work.

Then one day a minister hired him part-time to design advertisements for church events. It was hardly the opportunity of a lifetime, but he started working from a small shed behind the church, doing the drawings he was hired to produce, and also idly sketching whatever objects caught his eye.

Including the mice who scampered around the shed.

One of them, which one we'll never know, became the subject of a cartoon the artist named "Mickey." Eventually it became the most famous cartoon character in the world, and its creator, Walt Disney, became one of our century's most successful innovators of what is now known as "edutainment"—educational entertainment.

Somewhere within your sight and reach right now may lie some ordinary object that could transform your life. Can you recapture the magical thinking of a child and discover a treasure hidden nearby? It's worth taking a moment to find out, don't you think?

Success

"I know the plans I have for you," declares the Lord, "plans to prosper you and not to harm you, plans to give you hope and a future."

Jeremiah 29:11

True humility and respect for the Lord lead a man to riches, honor and long life.

Proverbs 22:4 TLB

They are like trees growing beside a stream, trees that produce fruit in season and always have leaves. Those people succeed in everything they do.

Psalm 1:3 CEV

Then the LORD your God will make you most prosperous in all the work of your hands and in the fruit of your womb, the young of your livestock and the crops of your land.

Deuteronomy 30:9

Who Gives You Your Dreams?

When Luciano Pavarotti was a little boy, he used to climb into his grandmother's lap, and she would tell him, "You're going to be great, you'll see." His grandmother's dream for him, however, was to become a banker!

Pavarotti started out as a schoolteacher, singing infrequently at special events. His father chided him for being so timid, and challenged him to develop the full potential of his voice.

At age twenty-two, Pavarotti stopped teaching, and fully committed himself to singing. He sold insurance part-time while he took voice lessons.

Now that he's one of the world's leading soloists, Pavarotti is happy to credit his voice teachers for his success. But he makes sure to add praise for his father and grandmother.

Alluding to his father, he says, "Studying voice was the turning point of my life. It's a mistake to take the safe path in life." Then he adds, with a twinkle in his eye, "My teachers groomed me. But no teacher ever told me I would become famous. Just my grandmother."

Someone in your life has given you a spark of confidence so you can achieve your best. And someone will give your children that same spark. Could it be you?

Suffering

Join with me in suffering for the gospel, by the power of God, who has saved us and called us to a holy life—not because of anything we have done but because of his own purpose and grace.

2 Timothy 1:8-9

I am sure that what we are suffering now cannot compare with the glory that will be shown to us.

Romans 8:18 CEV

Endure suffering along with me, as a good solider of Christ Jesus.

2 Timothy 2:3 NLT

When you do what is right and suffer for it you patiently endure it, this finds favor with God. For you have been called for this purpose, since Christ also suffered for you, leaving you an example for you to follow in His steps.

1 Peter 2:20-21 NASB

Ganging Up on Suffering

The "Hole in the Wall Gang Camp" is a very special place.

At first glance, you wouldn't notice its uniqueness. Opened in 1988, the camp is located on 300 acres of forest in northeastern Connecticut. Its rustic design resembles an Old West logging town of 100 years ago. Facilities feature a heated outdoor pool, boating, fishing, horseback riding, nature walks, woodworking, music, theater, crafts, and sports. Kids seven to seventeen attend four summer sessions.

But "Hole in the Wall" is special. For one thing, no camper is charged a fee. For another, it's the vision of actor Paul Newman and a group of dedicated volunteers. Then there's the fact that this camp accepts only children who have cancer, leukemia, and other serious blood diseases—children who, because of their illness, its treatment, or complications, cannot attend ordinary summer camps. These facilities are equipped to meet the medical and physical needs of these special children.

Suffering afflicts us in many ways. Some of it, unfortunately, we cannot avoid. But other suffering draws us together and helps us think creatively and act compassionately. When suffering enters your family's life, be assured there is much you can do to find physical and spiritual healing—together.

Suffering

Blessed be God, even the Father of our Lord Jesus Christ, the Father of mercies, and the God of all comfort; who comforteth us in all our tribulation, that we may be able to comfort them which are in any trouble, by the comfort wherewith we ourselves are comforted of God.

2 Corinthians 1:3-4 KJV

The Lord's people may suffer a lot, but he will always bring them safely through.

Psalm 34:19 CEV

Don't forget about those in prison. Suffer with them as though you were there yourself. Share the sorrow of those being mistreated, as though you feel their pain in your own bodies.

Hebrews 13:3 NLT

Our hope for you is firm, because we know that just as you share in our sufferings, so also you share in our comfort.

2 Corinthians 1:7

Sometimes You Can't Heal the Hurt

Five-year-old Charlie had a friend named Janie, who lived down the street. Every day Charlie asked to go play with Janie, and his mother nearly always permitted him to, but usually told him to come home at 6 o'clock.

One day 6 o'clock came and went, with no sign of Charlie. Then came 6:30, and 7, and finally when it was nearly dark Charlie came straggling into the house.

With a mixture of exasperation, fear, and relief, his mother scolded him and told him how worried she was and insisted he tell her why he was late.

Charlie explained that while they were playing, his friend Janie accidentally broke her doll.

"I see," said Charlie's mother. "So you were late because you helped Janie fix her doll?"

"Oh, no," Charlie replied. "I was helping her cry."

Many times when people are suffering, there is little we can do to heal their hurts. Physical pain from an illness, grief from death of a loved one, the numbness of the loss of a job—all may be beyond our inexpert abilities. But one thing we can always do is simply be there with the person, and for the person. All of us need somebody near to help us cry.

Temptation

Be self-controlled and alert. Your enemy the devil prowls around like a roaring lion looking for someone to devour. Resist him, standing firm in the faith, because you know that your brothers throughout the world are undergoing the same kind of sufferings.

1 Peter 5:8-9

The Lord knows how to deliver the godly out of temptations and to reserve the unjust under punishment for the day of judgment.

2 Peter 2:9 NKJV

Stay awake and pray that you won't be tested. You want to do what is right, but you are weak.

Mark 14:38 CEV

There is no creature hidden from His sight, but all things are open and laid bare to the eyes of Him with whom we have to do.

Hebrews 4:13 NASB

Somebody Always Sees

The father of a small boy would occasionally sneak over the fence into his neighbor's back yard and help himself to as much of the choicest fruit as he could carry in his shirt. He always made sure, however, that "the coast was clear."

One day his son tagged along. After carefully looking in every direction, and making sure his neighbor's car was gone, he crept over the fence, and helped his son to follow him.

Just as the father was about ready to help himself, his little boy whispered loudly, "Dad! Dad! Somebody's seeing us!"

"Where? Where?" the father answered. "I don't see anybody."

"You forgot to look up," his son explained. "You forgot to see if God is watching."

Temptation is a test of character, and character, they say, is what you do when you think nobody is watching. The spiritually mature person has learned to internalize the values of God's will, so it doesn't matter whether anyone is watching or not. Many spiritually immature people, however, try to perfect the ability to explain away their behavior, to manipulate the truth. Even a child, especially a child, can see that the coast is never clear enough to make a practice of yielding to temptation.

Temptation

No temptation has overtaken you that is not common to man. God is faithful, and he will not let you be tempted beyond your strength, but with the temptation will also provide the way of escape, that you may be able to endure it.

1 Corinthians 10:13 RSV

Since he himself has gone through suffering and temptation, he is able to help us when we are being tempted.

Hebrews 2:18 NLT

And lead us not into temptation, but deliver us from evil: For thine is the kingdom, and the power, and the glory, for ever. Amen.

Matthew 6:13 KJV

Consider him who endured such opposition from sinful men, so that you will not grow weary and lose heart. In your struggle against sin, you have not yet resisted to the point of shedding your blood.

Hebrews 12:3-4

Testing the Limits

Two hunting buddies had been flown into Canada's far North for some elk hunting. They stayed in a rustic cabin for a week, and waited triumphantly on their last day for the pilot to arrive to fly them out—with their bounty.

When the pilot had landed his plane, he inspected the proud hunters' six elk "I don't believe the plane will carry this many," he told them. "Four is about the limit."

"What about last year?" one of the hunters protested. "The pilot who carried us out then flew a plane that was exactly like this one—same horsepower, similar weather, and we had six elk then."

Reluctantly, the pilot agreed to try. They loaded up and took off, but sure enough there was insufficient power to take off. The plane sputtered as they tried to clear the mountains, and with all that weight, they crashed.

Stumbling bleeding from the wreckage, one hunter asked the other if he knew where they were.

"I'm not sure," he said, "but I think we're about two miles from where we crashed last year."

Some people never discover the true purpose of temptation—to help us learn that there are limits, beyond which lies only misfortune.

Truthfulness

Who may stay in God's temple or live on the holy mountain of the LORD? Only those who obey God and do as they should. They speak the truth and don't spread gossip; they treat others fairly and don't say cruel things.

Psalm 15:1-2 CEV

He is the Rock, His work is perfect; For all His ways are justice, A God of truth and without injustice; Righteous and upright is He.

Deuteronomy 32:4 NKJV

Buy truth, and do not sell it, Get wisdom and instruction and understanding.

Proverbs 23:23 NASB

Therefore each of you must put off falsehood and speak truthfully to his neighbor, for we are all members of one body.

Ephesians 4:25

A National Champion
in the Honesty Bee

Rosalie Elliott had made it to the fourth round of a national spelling contest in Washington. The eleven-year-old from South Carolina had been asked to spell the word *avowal*. In her soft southern accent she spelled the word, but the judges were not able to determine if she had used an *a* or an *e* as the next to last letter. They debated among themselves for several minutes as they listened to tape recording playbacks. The crucial letter, however, was too accent-blurred to decipher.

Finally the chief judge put the question to the only person who knew the answer. "Was the letter an *a* or was it an *e*?" he asked Rosalie.

By this time Rosalie had heard the correct spelling. Still, without hesitation, she replied that she had misspelled the word.

The entire audience stood and applauded, including some fifty news reporters. Even in defeat, she was a victor. Few remember the name of the first-place winner that year, but the name of Rosalie Elliott is passed down wherever stories about truthfulness are told.

Imagine the heartwarming and proud moment for Rosalie's parents! Our tests of truthfulness may be quite public, but we practice it in our ordinary family conversations.

Truthfulness

I have sinned and done wrong since the day I was born. But you want complete honesty, so teach me true wisdom.

Psalm 51:5-6 CEV

Speaking the truth in love, we will in all things grow up into him who is the Head, that is, Christ.

Ephesians 4:15

Love rejoices in the truth, but not in evil.

1 Corinthians 13:6 CEV

An honest witness tells the truth; a false witness tells lies.

Proverbs 12:17 NLT

Don't Look at Me in That Tone of Voice

An elderly Scottish couple who had never flown before decided to fly to America to see their grandchildren for the first time.

A couple of hours into the flight, they were high over the Atlantic when their pilot's voice came over the intercom:

"Ladies and gentlemen, I must let you know that one of our engines has failed. However, this is a three-engine jet, and it is entirely airworthy flying on two engines, but I regret to say I must slow our speed, so we will be one hour late arriving in New York."

Half an hour later, with an irritating calm the pilot spoke again: "I regret to inform you we have lost our second engine. We expect a normal and safe landing at JFK Airport. However, we shall be three hours late."

At this Grandma frowned, and with a hint of irritation in her voice said to Grandpa, "Dear me, if that third engine goes—we shall be up here all night."

We usually can tell when someone tries to cover the truth with a false tone of voice or an artificial gesture. So can children—so it's best to be completely truthful with them as soon as they're old enough and wise enough to understand.

Wisdom

Wisdom calls aloud outside; she raises her voice in the open squares.

Proverbs 1:20 NKJV

The fear of the Lord is the beginning of wisdom; all who follow his precepts have good understanding. To him belongs eternal praise.

Psalm 111:10

But you desire honestly from the heart, so you can teach me to be wise in my inmost being.

Psalm 51:6 NLT

O that ye would altogether hold your peace! and it should be your wisdom.

Job 13:5 KJV

Hard of Heeding

Jed Harris, the producer of *Our Town* and many other plays, became convinced he was losing his hearing. He went to a physician who couldn't find anything wrong, but he referred Harris to a specialist.

The specialist gave him a thorough checkup and nothing showed up to indicate a problem with his hearing. The doctor finally pulled a watch out of his pocket and asked, "Can you hear this ticking?"

Harris said, "Of course."

The specialist walked a few feet away and held up the watch again. "Now can you hear it?" he asked.

Harris concentrated and answered, "Yes, I can still hear it clearly."

Finally the doctor walked out the door of the examining room into the hallway and called, "Can you hear it now?"

Harris said, "Yes."

The specialist came back into the room and announced, "Mr. Harris, there is nothing wrong with your hearing. You just don't listen."

Sometimes the rush and distraction of our life renders us temporarily deaf to the wisdom that is available all around us. Our children, for example, are discovering the truths of life every day, and we might be amazed at what we can learn from them—when we listen.

Wisdom

To the man who pleases him, God gives wisdom,
knowledge and happiness.

Ecclesiastes 2:26

If you want to know what God wants you to do,
ask him, and he will gladly tell you, for he is
always ready to give a bountiful supply of wisdom
to all who ask him; he will not resent it.

James 1:5 TLB

Before Moses died, he had placed his hands on
Joshua, and the LORD had given Joshua wisdom.
The Israelites paid attention to what Joshua said
and obeyed the commands that the LORD had
given Moses.

Deuteronomy 34:9 CEV

Wisdom is with aged men, With long life is
understanding. With Him are wisdom and might;
To Him belong counsel and understanding.

Job 12:12-13 NASB

Knowing When To Quit

Sir Winston Churchill spent three years in the eighth grade because he had trouble learning English. Years later, after he had become one of the twentieth century's greatest orators, Oxford University asked him to address its commencement exercises.

The packed audience arose in appreciative applause as he approached the podium with his famous top hat, cane, and cigar. With great dignity Churchill settled the crowd as he stood confidently before his expectant admirers.

Looking directly at the eager audience, and with the authority that came with being the leader of his country's World War II victory ringing in his voice, he began with these words:

"Never give up!" he cried.

Several seconds passed. He rocked back and forth and then shouted again:

"Never give up!" he thundered.

Profound silence met his words as they rolled across the audience. Churchill then reached for his hat and his cigar, steadied himself with his cane, and left the platform. His address was finished.

Churchill's six-word address was no doubt the shortest and most eloquent ever delivered at Oxford. Surely it is one of the most memorable.

Wisdom involves both knowing the right thing to say—and when to stop saying it.

Work

When God gives any man wealth and possessions, and enables him to enjoy them, to accept his lot and be happy in his work—this is a gift of God.

Ecclesiastes 5:19

"Don't work for food that spoils. Work for food that gives eternal life. The Son of Man will give you this food, because God the Father has given him the right to do so."

John 6:27 CEV

God is not unfair. He will not forget how hard you have worked for him and how you have shown your love to him by caring for other Christians, as you still do.

Hebrews 6:10 NLT

Work hard and cheerfully at all you do, just as though you were working for the Lord and not merely for your masters, remembering that it is the Lord Christ who is going to pay you, giving you your full portion of all he owns. He is the one you are really working for.

Colossians 3:23-24 TLB

Operas and Overalls

A famous opera singer was visited by her brother, who showed up at the concert hall wearing a hard hat, coveralls, and boots. As he was waiting for his renowned sister to finish her rehearsal, one of the opera company actors engaged him in well-meaning conversation.

"You must be proud to have a sister who is known around the world for her singing talent," the actor said. Then, looking more closely at the man's clothing, he added insult to injury by saying, "Of course, not everyone in the same family has to have the same amount of talent."

"You're right," the carpenter said. "For example, my sister doesn't know the first thing about building a house. She's lucky she can afford to pay me to build a home for her. That's why I'm here—to go over the plans I've designed."

This man (and probably his sister also) knew what Booker T. Washington used to teach, that "there is as much dignity in tilling a field as in writing a poem." One of the most valuable gifts we can give our children is the joy of fully believing in our work, whatever vocation we may have chosen.

Work

Even when we were with you, we gave you this rule: "If a man will not work, he shall not eat."
2 Thessalonians 3:10

Each man's work will become evident; for the day will show it, because it is to be revealed with fire; and the fire itself will test the quality of each man's work.
1 Corinthians 3:13 NASB

God has promised us a Sabbath when we will rest, even though it has not yet come. On that day God's people will rest from their work, just as God rested from his work.
Hebrews 4:9-10 CEV

Six days shall work be done: but the seventh day is the sabbath of rest, and holy convocation; ye shall do no work therein: it is the sabbath of the LORD in all your dwellings.
Leviticus 23:3 KJV

Even God Rested

A management consultant makes the following observation:

"Be the first in the office every morning, be the last to leave every night, never take a day off, slave through the lunch hour, and the inevitable day will come when the boss will summon you to his office and say,

"I've been watching your work very carefully, Jackson. Just what the devil are you up to anyhow?"

We are in such a hurry to succeed, to pack each moment with adventure, that we don't leave ourselves any time to enjoy, to reflect, to rejoice, to be grateful, to rest. We are encouraged to learn to take a sabbath rest. In a 1998 book by Naomi Levy, *TO BEGIN AGAIN: The Journey Toward Comfort, Strength, and Faith in Difficult Times*, she writes: "The Bible views rest as a divine activity; not as a sign of laziness or weakness but as a sign of holiness and wisdom."

As fathers, we're often urged to offer our children an example of how to be successful at work. But equally important is our mandate to show them how to make spiritually helpful use of their leisure time—to "remember the Sabbath, and keep it holy."

Additional copies of this book and other titles from
Honor Books are available from your local bookstore:

God's Little Lessons on Life
God's Little Lessons for Mothers
God's Little Lessons for Graduates
God's Little Lessons for Parents
God's Little Lessons for Teachers
God's Little Lessons for Teens
God's Little Lessons for Leaders
God's Little Lessons for Women

If you have enjoyed this book, or if it has
impacted your life, we would like to hear from you.
Please contact us at:

Honor Books

4050 Lee Vance View

Colorado Springs, CO 80918

www.cookministries.com